P9-CRI-055

A Study of Self-Deception

A Study of Self-Deception

M.R. HAIGHT

Lecturer in Philosophy, University of Glasgow

THE HARVESTER PRESS · SUSSEX

HUMANITIES PRESS · NEW JERSEY

First published in Great Britain in 1980 by
THE HARVESTER PRESS LIMITED
Publishers: John Spiers and Margaret A. Boden
16 Ship Street, Brighton, Sussex
and in the USA by
HUMANITIES PRESS INC.,
Atlantic Highlands, New Jersey 07716

© M.R. Haight, 1980

British Library Cataloguing in Publication Data
Haight, Mary
   A study of self-deception.
   1. Self-deception
   I. Title
   153   BF697

ISBN 0–85527–918–4

Humanities Press Inc.
ISBN 0–391–01803–5

Typeset by Inforum Ltd, Portsmouth
Printed in Great Britain by
Redwood Burn Limited, Trowbridge and Esher

CONTENTS

Preface   vii
Preliminary Note   xi
Sonnet CXXXVIII   xii

1   Stories that Leave Something Out   1
2   A Linguistic Five-Finger Exercise   8
3   Selves that Can Deceive Each Other   24
4   Philonous and Hylas on Dissociation   37
5   Bad Faith and Some Alternatives   53
6   Strategy and Tactics   73
7   A Change of Map?   89
8   Self-Deceivers and Other People   108
9   The Judge and the Social Worker   120

Appendix A   (1) Sources for Case Histories
(Multiple Personality)   133
(2) The 'Split Brain' Model for
Self-Deception   136
Appendix B   (1) 'Virtue is Knowledge'   142
(2) 'If You Knew, You Were
Responsible'   147

Notes   150
Short Bibliography   157
Index of Proper Names and Pseudonyms   159
Index of Subjects   161

For Justine Chase Ashby
and George Haight

PREFACE

How will you look for something when you don't in the least know what it is?
How on earth are you going to set up something you don't know as the object
of your search? To put it another way, even if you come right up against it,
how will you know that what you have found is the thing you didn't know?
(Plato: *Meno* 80d, tr. Guthrie)

What is self-deception? There are examples which (I think)
most people who use the word would call typical. You will find
some in this book: C the man who may have cancer, ignoring his
symptoms or explaining them away; D the drinking man who,
in the teeth of the evidence, will not admit he is on the way to
alcoholism; M the doting mother, blind to her son's faults in a
way that does not really seem possible; S the scientist who
maintains — blandly, as though it needed no defense — that
what may result from his research in biological warfare is no
affair of his. But to call cases typical is not to show understanding, if we cannot clearly say what they are typical of.

Philosophers (to avoid some form of the *Meno* problem) often
insist that they do not study things, only concepts or the language that embodies them. The only flaws in understanding
which a philosopher is then licensed to discover are those that
conceptual analysis shows up: incoherence, emptiness and so
on. And we must start with that, certainly. It is our concept of
self-deception that leads us to pick as typical the cases I have
mentioned, instead of others which we call (more leniently)
wishful thinking or (more cynically) *pretence*. But analysis of
what we call them — which might be expected to show what we
think they are — in fact shows rather quickly that whatever they
are, self-deceivers cannot literally be *that*: 'self-deception' con-
tradicts itself. (See Chapter 2.) We have then, on the one
hand, a type (or types) of behaviour that we can recognize; on
the other, we have a name which is paradoxical, as though
literal language failed us here. Why?

At this point we need not conceptual analysis but fact: *what is really going on?* This is still the study of concepts in a way; but search and synthesis are as important as analysis. We need to investigate what is likely, as well as what is logically possible. And this needs a different kind of example: not types prejudged by our (now clearly inadequate) concept, but individuals — biographical, autobiographical, clinical, fictional too when the author seems to draw from life. Some of the most illuminating may also be people we never would call self-deceivers, but who do, in an evident or extreme way, things that self-deceivers also *might* do. The most picturesque are probably the multiple personality cases in Chapter 3: Christine Beauchamp, Christine Sizemore ('Eve' of *The Three Faces of Eve*), and so forth. A theory of self-deception must (I think) depend on a theory of consciousness, and no theory of consciousness can ignore cases like these. But they are only part of a much wider range. From all this, a pattern begins to form of what self-deception may really be.

There are very few existing full-scale theories of self-deception. If I had found an adequate one, I would not have written this book. Each of the main ones has (I shall argue) serious flaws which are conceptual, so that it would be possible to dismiss them on logical grounds alone. But once again this is surely not enough: a theory may be incoherent and still — for its richness, its piecemeal truths and suggestive part-truths — one we ought to study. I shall discuss three at some length: the Freudian, the Existentialist, and Fingarette's theory of disavowal.

The last part of this book is less about 'What?' than 'Why?': why should we have and seem to need so paradoxical a concept, given what (I think) really goes on? The answer seems to be that if we don't look into it too carefully, we may think that it helps us to resolve certain dilemmas in judging action: problems of freedom, responsibility, blame; of the Socratic paradox; and of what I call the 'Judge's Rule': '*If you knew, you were responsible*'. We are caught between rival theories of action, a 'hard line' and a 'soft'. I personify them in Chapter 9 as a Judge and a Social Worker endlessly disputing (for which I apologize to all real social workers and judges who are not so stereotyped). But once looked into, the concept's easy usefulness is lost; and so it should be, since it only masks the problems. If there is any way to solve them, it cannot be by pretending that the impossible is real.

I would like to thank Wilma White and Anne Valentine, who typed a good deal of this book in one version or another, and the following people who read all or some of it at some time before it was published, and gave encouragement, useful criticism and good advice which I have not always followed: Justine Chase Ashby, Dr Nicholas Bunnin, Professor R.S. Downie, Michael Lessnoff, Professor G.E.L. Owen, Professor Eva Schaper, Janet Sisson.

PRELIMINARY NOTE

When I gave this book to someone who was not an academic philosopher to read, the only convention that she found puzzling was my way of using letters for propositions, with or without a negation sign. So to explain: I often make a letter (generally 'p') stand for a proposition or statement which we would typically express by a sentence: 'The sun is a star' for example. We may use various sentences to make the same statement: 'Sol is a star' (in this case) or 'That is a star' (in context, and I think that context is always a factor). 'It is true that p' may therefore stand for 'It is true that the sun is a star', 'Patricia knows that p' for 'Patricia knows that the sun is a star', and so forth.

With cognitive terms like 'know' and 'believe', referential opacity may complicate things. Patricia may know that the sun is a star for example without (in one sense) knowing that Sol is a star, if she does not know that 'Sol' names the sun. And referential opacity can, I think, play a part in self-deceptive manoeuvres (see Chapter 6: we may at times accept one way of putting a truth when we will not face another, even when it seems that we must somehow know they refer to the same thing). But this should not confuse my use of 'p' for propositions known, believed and so on, so long as the reader keeps it in mind that such questions of interpretation may always arise.

I use a *tilde* ('∼') for negation. The safe translation of it is 'It is not the case that . . .', but before 'p' we may read it simply as 'Not . . .' ('Patricia believes that not-p'); and any given sentence in English will have its own more colloquial negations ('Everybody likes chocolate'/'Not everybody likes chocolate'; 'The sun is a star'/'The sun is not a star'). I sometimes use 'p*' for a proposition that is not, but is closely related to, p (see Chapter 1); and I often use 'p' not for a single more or less simple proposition but for some open-ended set of them: we may think of them as joined by words like 'and'. Any other variations should be clear in the context.

SONNET CXXXVIII

When my love swears that she is made of truth,
I do believe her, though I know she lies;
That she may think me some untutor'd youth,
Unlearned in the world's false subtleties.
Thus vainly thinking that she thinks me young,
Although she knows my days are past the best,
Simply I credit her false-speaking tongue;
On both sides thus is simple truth supprest.
But wherefore says she not she is unjust?
And wherefore say I not that I am old?
O, love's best habit is in seeming trust,
And age in love loves not to have years told:
    Therefore I lie with her, and she with me,
    And in our faults by lies we flatter'd be.

William Shakespeare

1 STORIES THAT LEAVE SOMETHING OUT

SELF-DECEPTION is an odd idea: it seems paradoxical. Yet we have no simpler name for what we take it to be, and we use the name we have as if its meaning were not in doubt. Later I shall argue that the paradox is real, with no way round it, so that the name — whatever we mean by it — cannot literally mean *that*. But I shall start with a sketch of the kind of thing we call by that name and, by contrast, some things that are like it but not the same.

Self-deception is not mere wishful thinking. Béla Szabados makes the point clearly in his paper 'Wishful Thinking and Self-Deception'[1]: if I call a man's belief wishful thinking I need not even imply that it is false. But I must mean this if I say that he deceives himself. The wishful thinker believes on too little evidence, the self-deceiver 'in the teeth of the evidence. . . . In self-deceit the evidence is *against* the belief held. Once this is pointed out to the person involved, if he then proceeds to resist, by ingenious tactics, the natural implications of the evidence, we feel that he is self-deceived'[2]. The 'ingenious tactics' here are presumably behaviour and speech: we cannot read the self-deceiver's mind. But even so he is clearly trying somehow, as Szabados says, to pervert the procedures by which we establish truth and falsehood. A wishful thinker need not be perverse, only self-indulgent.

But I do not think that this means we can never do both at once. If I call a thing wishful thinking, I suggest that it is not self-deception; but only because I use a weak term where, if it fitted, we would expect a strong one. In fact self-deception seems to entail wishful thinking. If I deceive myself so as to believe that a certain proposition (p) is true, I do it (we usually suppose) in order not to face some real and unwelcome truth. My belief that p is what allows me to do this, so p is what I wish to think; and I lack good grounds for thinking it. But I add what makes it self-deception: grounds against p, which I resist. This explains why we may feel that self-deception shades into wishful thinking, with no clear line between them: it can be hard to say at what point the facts begin to show not just a lack of evidence for p, but evidence against it.

Self-deception might be called wishful thinking grown stubborn and perverse. When we blame wishful thinking it is as a kind of negligence: a failure to take account of the weakness of one's case. We may in the same way blame other failures that lead to unjustified belief; but so long as the believer is only negligent, I think that we would not call it self-deception. Here is an example that brings in a good many failures of this kind.

A Sunday paper asks me to write a story about the early life of famous Uncle Henry. I need the money, so I write it — to the distress of his widow Aunt Emily, who thinks it a betrayal of privacy. I am sorry. I never thought she would take it that way. But I should have thought so: I am to blame for various kinds of negligence. I was (1) insensitive (I never thought that it would worry her, because it would not worry *me*); (2) careless and lazy (I did not trouble to write and ask permission); (3) gullible, due to wishful thinking (their daughter Margaret said 'What fun! Mind you send a copy to Mummy!' and I took this at face value); (4) forgetful (I should have remembered how Aunt Emily hated a story like that about someone else) — and so on. The pattern is of thought and trouble avoided for unworthy reasons; and no doubt I would have taken the trouble and thought if I had really wanted to know. On the other hand, it is still quite likely that if finding out what Aunt Emily felt had been easier to do than not, I would have done it; and then I would have given up the story because I would rather not hurt Aunt Emily.

To say that I deceived myself would be to throw doubt on just that point; and we would have reason to doubt it if — but only if — the unworthy reasons that I mentioned do not seem quite enough to explain what I did. Suppose for example: (1) I'm suddenly taking a tougher line on what I would or would not mind people knowing about me. (2) I often use the University library in the town where Aunt Emily lives, and then I nearly always have tea with her and tell her my news. Exceptionally, I have been to the library only once these six weeks, and somehow I forgot to tell her that I was coming. So I did not go to see her. (3) It was odd of me to stop and talk with Cousin Margaret. Usually I avoid her. She is silly and vain and always malicious about her charming, clever parents. (4) I did think once or twice of the memoir that Aunt Emily hated, but somehow I had the idea that it was more revealing than what I meant to write. I could have checked of course — it is somewhere on my shelves — but somehow I never found the time. And so on. The 'somehows' may be filled with reasons, each likely enough on its own; but now the pattern is not of trouble shirked, but of means to an end: not to see what stared me in the face.

My wish in either case could be the same: to sell my story, undisturbed by conscience. My aim in each is therefore to believe the same groundless thing. But it is worse than groundless in the case that we would call self-deception: here I need *and seem to know that I need* positively to suppress the truth.

At a different border self-deception shades into delusion: I mean the delusion that we think typical of madness, not the kind where one man is said to delude another. To say 'A is deluded' is like calling him self-deceived, in that it says his beliefs are false and (by normal standards) unreasonable. The schizophrenic who believes that he is seeing God does so in the teeth of evidence that makes other people call him mad. Moreover, unless it is clearly due to some outside cause like a drug, we think that delusions are caused by something about the man who has them.

We might therefore call madmen *self*-deluded, but we do not; or if ever we do, it suggests that the delusion is part self-deception; perhaps began with it. What self-deception has and delusion lacks, I think, is an air of responsibility or choice: we may feel this even when the delusion too looks like the means to some end.

To point the difference: hallucination in itself is neither delusion nor its opposite; it is simply a perceptual state. A madman may believe strange things of what he 'hears' or 'sees' where a sane one would not. This is common enough when hallucination comes from a drug or a fever, or when a dream runs into waking. It once happened to me: I opened my eyes and say my window against the dark, but for a while I also saw the thing that had been strangling me in my dream. I seemed to read the dim square of light before my eyes now as the window and now as it. But I knew that the window was real and it was not.

We may then be deluded or realistic about hallucination; we may also deceive ourselves. Suppose that the leader of a cult gives his people a 'sacramental cup' and they see visions. One of them is a doctor. He has every reason to know that they come from a drug in the wine; he may even be able to guess which; but he will not allow that this is possible.

In fact we may find all three attitudes — realism about hallucination, or delusion, or self-deception — in the schizophrenic. I know one who often assesses his visions as we would: they seem to come from God (he says) but the evidence is against it. At other times he seems deluded. And since they can be grander and more beautiful (he says) than anything in ordinary life, we may suppose that he sometimes assesses them self-deceivingly, choosing to believe in the teeth of what he knows to be evidence against them.

Several philosophers have tried to avoid the paradox that such perversity implies — or seems to imply — by weakening the concept: they play down the self-deceiver's command of evidence against his belief, or the way that he seems to *choose* not to know the truth, or his final success. Then to bring back all that 'self-deception' in fact suggests, they hedge, and either bring back the paradox without noticing it or equivocate between paradox and something less than what the term means. Herbert Fingarette discusses such theses at length in his book *Self-Deception*[3] and where he is critical I tend to agree; so I shall myself quote only one of this kind (an interesting one) to show what I mean.

Raphael Demos uses 'lie', not 'deceive', in his title 'On Lying to Oneself'[4] so as not to forget that we commonly hold self-deceivers responsible; he then uses an analogy that forgets it. Lying to oneself, he says, is like not noticing a headache during an interesting film (not to be confused with taking aspirin so that the headache goes away). He takes the example of a mother who lies to herself about her worthless son, and concludes:

There is an impulse favouring one belief at the expense of its contradictory; and the person who lies to himself, because of yielding to impulse, fails to notice or ignores what he knows to be the case. Such an analysis 'saves' the phenomena while at the same time conforming to the requirements of the law of contradiction. For, indeed, we are saying that the person who lies to himself believes p and ~p, and is capable of doing so because he is distracted by the former. Finally this account is not far different from the way in which people express the fact in ordinary language. Thus they would say of the mother who has come to believe that her son is a fine fellow, that she knows all along *in a corner of her mind* that he is not much good.[5]

I would say about this: (1) The ordinary saying (for what it is worth) is that the mother *knows* that her son is not much good; this need not entail belief. She might know that ~p and believe that p ('My son is a fine fellow') without confusion, just because she does *not* believe that ~p: what she knows is temporarily forgotten, perhaps (in the Freudian sense) repressed. I shall say more about this use of 'know' later; all I need to say here is that this is the kind of thing 'in a corner of her mind' might refer to. If we (rightly) call this *failing to notice* what she knows — and would normally, if she noticed it, believe — there is indeed no paradox; but this is because failing to notice is *prima facie* not deliberate. And if it happens to be due to repression, it is not even clearly an omission that we can blame. (2) Demos also says however that she *ignores a belief* that ~p. This is to say something more. 'Ignore' means '*choose* not to notice', where 'notice' is active too: not just 'observe' but 'acknowledge that one observes'. (Demos' 'yielding to impulse' gets by because it is vague enough to fit both 'does not observe' and 'ignores', though I think it favours the second.) If I ignore a headache, I deliberately turn my thoughts to other things. Probably I hope that this will either stop my noticing the headache or will make it go away. *Not to notice it* will be to be aware of something or other that tells me I would feel it, if I were not being distracted: heaviness, throbbing, a pang if I jerk my head; otherwise I have no reason not to say that the headache goes away during the film and later comes back. I can think of only one other possibility: (I shall say more about this later): we may perhaps sometimes remember or 'remember' a thing recorded when we were not conscious of it. If so, I might become aware now that the physical state I usually feel as a headache was there when I watched the film, while also remembering that at the time I did not feel it.

But however we take it, the headache is a bad analogy for self-deception without paradox. If I do not feel it at the time, 'not noticing' must be taken as in (1). It can mean more than this only if the sufferer deliberately makes himself unaware of it, which would be most unusual: headache sufferers would do it if they could. On the other hand, if I do feel (say) a pang as I jerk my head, the self-deceiving mother will by analogy be aware from time to time of something that tells her *she would believe that* ~p if she paid attention — or at the very least, that she might. But this is to be aware that she may have reason to believe that ~p. The only exception to this would be a case where ~p is some belief, more emotional than epistemological, for she knows there are no grounds — as she might know, walking in the graveyard at night, that if she does not distract herself she may come to think Something is following her. In Demos' example, however, she cannot know that she has no grounds: *ex hypothesi* she has. We may go so far as to suppose that they too are repressed, so that she is not aware of them; but if she is aware of anything at all that will make her case like the headache one, this is enough to bring back the paradox.

And surely the headache analogy is right on this point. She must be aware at least of something that tells her — to put it as vaguely as we can — '*I may have reason to believe something bad about my son*' (call this p*); for she must care greatly about her son's character, or the example fails for lack of motive. And p* is so relevant to this that it seems impossible she could be distracted. (So where p* is concerned 'ignore' must be right, not 'fail to notice'.) But to choose, she must be aware of the alternatives — to distract herself from p* or not — and so she must be aware that p*. That is, she is not distracted from it. The paradox of self-deception seems only to have moved a step back.

Usually however we need not bother with the extra step. If she is to ignore the original ~p ('My son is not much good') the mother must know where not to look. This is why p* cannot be simply '*I may have reason to believe something unpleasant*'. She must seem to pay normal attention to what her son says and does, and to what people say or hint about him, or she gives the game away. But the better she selects, the more it looks as though she knows not only that p*, but that ~p. As Sartre says in *Being and Nothingness*, '. . . I must know the truth very exactly *in order* to conceal it more carefully. . . . How then can the lie subsist, if the duality which conditions it is suppressed?"[6]

2 A LINGUISTIC FIVE-FINGER EXERCISE

IF we really cannot lie to ourselves, we speak in metaphor whenever we accuse someone of doing it. 'Deceive oneself' is no better. We blame people for it, suggest that they stop doing it, in short we treat self-deception as an act just as lying is an act. There are weaker senses of 'deceive' ('The clear air deceived me — I thought the hills were closer!') but they will not bear the concept's weight. But if a metaphor means anything, we should also be able to say it literally. My first chapter suggests that any other account which seems complete must keep the paradox, and so be no less metaphorical. So I want to consider in detail what this paradox is which (it seems) we cannot do without.

If to deceive oneself is really to deceive, a definition of 'A deceives B' should fit some cases where B and A are the same, and these should be the cases that in fact we call 'self-deception'. For I think that 'deceives' (unlike 'art' or 'game') is definable. Typically, if A deceives B, then *for some proposition or propositions p, A knows that p; and* (with two qualifications) *A keeps B from knowing that p*. This need not mean that A or B can put p into words: 'p' stands for the proposition(s) that anyone might put into words, who stated the fact(s) A is hiding.

The qualifications are these. (1) Usually when A deceives B he does indeed keep B from knowing that p — which is to say that B would know it, but for him. This must be so if A deceives B by hiding evidence, or by keeping silent when B would expect anyone who knew that p to speak out. But I might tell a child 'Come in before dark or the Grasshopper Witch will get you!' He believes me; I have deceived him. But it would be wrong to say that, but for me, he would now know something that he does not. But for me, he would not have thought of a Grasshopper Witch at all. We should say here that A deceives B by *making B believe a thing which A knows to be false*, and so change our definition to read: if A deceives B, then *for some propo-*

sition(s) p, A knows that p; and either A keeps B from knowing that p, or A makes B believe that ~p, or (very likely) *both.* (2) So far we have taken it that A alone deceives B. But he could also be just one of many delusive reasons why B does not know that p or believes that ~p, or both, so that even if A were not there B would be deceived. Perhaps even if A were to tell him the truth, the other things or people might not let B believe it. Still if A does not tell him, but connives at the illusion either by omission (say a timely silence) or commission (say a lie), he too deceives B. If B were later to charge him with it on these grounds, we would agree that the charge was just. So we should really, and finally, say: if A deceives B, then *for some proposition(s) p, A knows that p; and either A keeps or helps it to keep B from knowing that p, or A make or helps to make B believe that ~p, or both.* This is clumsy when spelled out, but the clumsiness does not matter. What matters is that at any time when A decieves B, A — to deceive — must know that p, when B — when deceived — must not.

Deceptions can last for some time. When they last any time at all, A's knowledge and B's ignorance overlap; but if B is A this seems impossible. It does not help that 'A knows that p' must nearly always be taken in a dispositional sense (A would not have p forever in mind). If it has this sense, 'B does not know that p' will mean that B lacks that same disposition — so the paradox will remain.

We can try to resolve it in two ways. We might look for a wider sense of 'A deceives B'; or we might treat 'A' in self-deception, where A deceives A, as equivocal, the 'A' and 'B' roles to be taken by different aspects of one person. The first way is simpler and better if we can do it, since names mean whole people unless we have special reason to deny it. So first I shall try, *without redefining 'A'*, to stretch the meaning of 'deceive' beyond my *prima facie* plausible definition. We might do this by recasting A's role in 'A deceives B', or B's role, or both.

A's role, however, seems essential. If A does not know that p, then either p is false, or p is true but A has not got grounds for it. (1) Suppose that p is false. B of course is then not misled by anyone who 'hides' p from him or makes him believe that ~p (etc.). A may *mean* to deceive B. This would justify B if (for example) he wanted to call A deceitful. But B is never actually deceived. (2) Suppose that A himself is not sure of p. Then if he denies it he may be telling the truth, for all he knows, and if he supresses it he may only be suppressing a lie. *Deliberate* deceivers must (I think) know better what they are doing, so (2) is no more use than (1). If A is not sure of p he can of course still *accidentally* deceive or *mislead* B about p, in many kinds of bad faith; but this is not quite enough.

Something else that need not trouble us here is the question 'How can A be sure that he has (or sure that he lacks) grounds for p?' For my definition did not say 'If A deceives B *about p*, then A knows that p . . .' (etc.). The p in question may be only obliquely related to the main deception. In one of the stories about the notorious Mullah Nasrudin, the Mullah tells his villagers for a joke that there is gold buried in a certain field. They rush off to dig. Suddenly he takes a spade and goes to join them, because after all it might be true. Since the story really might be true, '*There is no gold in that field*' cannot be p. But Nasrudin knows that *there is none, for all Nasrudin knows*. He has let the villagers think the reverse, so this can be p; and if there were no such p they could not fairly accuse him of deceiving them. In this story they certainly can. In short, some p of this kind will always exist when A deceives B, whatever else is involved. For A's private view of the topic of deception *must somehow be different from the one he shows to B, and A must know in what way it is so*. Otherwise he cannot mean to deceive.

A's effect on B has to be deliberate. Suppose that Nasrudin's story also gives people the idea that the Mullah has already taken some treasure home. If he never meant them to think this, its negation is not a possible p: they have misunderstood, not been deceived in this respect. It might indeed be the last thing he wanted them to think: they will dig up his garden and ransack his house and find a few things whose disappearance from other houses has not as yet (he hopes) been traced to him . . . .

So it seems that for A the account that I gave must stand: he must know that p. Now for B. A must keep or help to keep B from some attitude to p; but might it not be a weaker one then knowledge, or anyway different? Or A must make or help to make B take some positive attitude to ~p; but might this not be one that still allows B to know that p? Or A might of course do both.

I shall take each possibility in turn. We cannot say in the first case that A keeps B from *accepting* that p, or any other verb that means B is kept only from behaving or feeling as if p were true. People can act or feel the wrong things in cases which nevertheless they understand. We need something stronger. On the other hand, we cannot say that A keeps B from *admitting* or *acknowledging* that p, for this means admitting (etc.) *the truth* of p — in other words, that p is known. By the same argument we cannot say in the second case that A only makes or helps to make B act as if ~p. He could do these and be aware all the time that p, in which case he is not deceived. Nor can we say that A makes or helps to make B acknowledge or recognize or admit that ~p, unless we contradict ourselves, for we have assumed that ~p is false

Both 'accept' (etc.) and 'admit' (etc.) are used of those we call self-deceivers: 'He knows but he won't admit it, even to himself'; 'He knows, but he won't accept it'. But we also hear from Shakespeare,

When my love swears that she is made of truth
I do believe her, though I know she lies[7]

or from Rebecca West, 'We all knew that Papa would not write, yet for some time we believed that he would',[8] and other combinations of '*believe*' with 'know' to mean self-deception or something like it. 'Believe' has a wide range: it covers both the too-weak 'accept' and the too-strong 'admit', so that we might hope to find a middle sense of the term that is strong enough for 'A deceives B' without making it impossible for A to deceive A. Let us try (for the first kind of deception) the definition '*A knows that p, and A keeps or helps to keep B from believing that p*', for some sense of 'believe' that we have yet to find.

This means that we must decide about the relation between belief and knowledge; for if knowing that p entails believing that p the trial obviously fails. Many philosophers think that it does, and with one exception so do I. To put it briefly, arguments that this is not so usually appeal to two things. One is the fact that in common usage 'A believes that p' has the force of 'A does not know that p'. (Either p is false or A lacks evidence.)

The other is a general difference in kind between 'know' (a capacity or achievement term) and 'believe' (a motive term) — the distinction made for example by Gilbert Ryle in *The Concept of Mind*.[9]

Of these, the first is easily answered. If we say it shows that knowing that p and believing that p are not compatible, we confuse Gricean 'conversational implicature' with implication in the strict sense: we claim that what 'A believes that p' conveys when stated, without special qualification, in most contexts, must follow from any such statement wherever it occurs. With the second I have more sympathy. Certainly to know *how* (that is, to have a skill) seems far enough in meaning from 'believe' to make it unlikely that 'know' implies a corresponding 'believe' every time. One may also, as I have already said, *know that p* (in the epistemological sense) and not believe that p, where 'believe' means only 'act or feel as though p'. But when 'believe' is epistemological too, the first does seem to entail the second. My argument for this would follow the lines (for example) of A.J. Ayer's in *The Problem of Knowledge*.[10] There is a joke: 'The man's such a liar, I wouldn't believe him even when I *knew* he was telling the truth!'; it is only a joke for this reason. But there is one exception, and it will allow the account of 'deceive' that we want: one could keep A from believing that p by putting his *knowledge* that p temporarily out of reach.

Suppose a demagogue (Colonel A) converts B. B shows clear signs of believing all that A says, which means that B must believe some proposition(s)~p. B asserts this, campaigns for A on these grounds, and so on, with utter sincerity. ~p presupposes, however, that something B has known for years (p) is false. He has first-class evidence (being an eye-witness perhaps) but seems to have forgotten it entirely. However we describe B now, he does not seem to believe that p — quite the reverse. Then suppose that something reminds him of what he has seen, and it dawns on him that ~p is false and that he has always been in a position to show it. 'You see how dangerous A is' he says. '*I knew quite well all the time that p*, but until I remembered xyz, he had me believing the opposite!'

There are reasons for taking this seriously. A makes B believe that ~p and, while it lasts, this keeps B from believing that p. B has evidence that shows ~p is false, and it is not simply that he fails to make the connection: he is not aware that he has it. We still have the following reasons for saying that B knows all the time that p: (1) He has learned that p. (2) He does not need to learn that p again; he recalls it. (3) Nothing during the time when he believes ~p makes him unable *a priori* to know that p. He has not become senile or dead, his brain is not damaged (etc). (4) To be said to know that p, we need not always be able to state p when p is to the point, even on demand. We may try and fail to remember something we *know* that we know ('I was discussing it with Soandso just this morning'); we may even think that we do not know something and later remember that we do.

Of these points, (1), (3) and (4) suggest that we *may* say B knows all the time that p, unless we insist that '*Knowing that p entails believing that p*' is an axiom, which is surely going too far. And (2) gives a reason why we *should*.

Of course we must not simply say 'B, while enthralled by Colonel A, knows that p' and leave it at that. This makes it incredible that B should also disbelieve that p, at least for any sense of 'believe' strong enough to let us say that B is deceived. His disbelief after all consists of this: throughout his infatuation *he believes that ~p* and therefore fails to act, speak, feel, think like a man who knows that p, as 'knows' is generally understood. We need to distinguish ordinary knowledge from knowledge that is buried. This is too simple, of course. In our story p comes back to B when something stirs his memory, and I might even have made him remember spontaneously, so far as anyone can tell. Such things happen. But other memories might be buried deeper. Still we can roughly call knowledge buried if it is not recalled when recollection is to be expected. Though buried, it is still knowledge, so long as nothing makes recall impossible. Something may of course do this without giving any sign; in fact the only sure proof that knowledge is buried and not lost comes when we later recall it. But for my argument all we need to know is that knowledge can be buried, and that when this happens we may stop believing what we know.

Allow that, and we still need one more thing to make this a story of A deceiving B: Colonel A too must know that ~p is false. That could be. But his knowledge (which amounts to knowing that p) cannot also be buried. Imagine A in the bemused state we gave to B — asserting, campaigning and so on in all sincerity — and we can charge A at most with deceiving B unintentionally, or misleading him. He will only have made B believe what he believes himself.

But one man's knowledge cannot be both buried and not buried. (From now on I shall use 'free' to mean 'not buried'.) So not even the formula 'A puts B's knowledge out of his reach' will fit *self*-deception. This holds for the second part of my definition too ('*A knows that p, and makes or helps to make B believe that ~p*'). In fact the demagogue story is a case of both.

I think that this argument is sound so far as it goes, but it leaves two loopholes. I took it that any deception must last for some time, however short; and deceptions usually do. But perhaps some do not, and perhaps these include self-deceptions. Since this is really a case where 'A' is equivocal (past A deceives present A) I shall leave it for the moment. I also assumed that when we take 'A believes that p' to mean that A has a certain disposition, we must take 'A does not believe that p' to mean that A lacks this same disposition, so that one or the other must be true of A and both cannot be true at once. I think that this is how we usually mean dispositional terms. But the logic of the dispositional terms 'know' and 'believe' is not so clear that we may take it for granted they will fit the usual rules.

The distinction between free and buried knowledge comes to this. A's knowledge that p is buried if and only if *A knows that p, but his knowledge does not lead to a belief that p*. I put it this way rather than just 'A knows but does not believe that p' because one might combine buried knowledge with free belief, if the belief were based on other grounds than what one knows. A child might see his father kill his mother, bury the memory deep, and later come to believe that his father must have killed his mother because of things that his foster-parents hinted. And A knows freely that p if and only if *A knows that p and his knowledge leads to belief*. What the two forms of knowledge share is non-dispositional: A has learned that p, and he is not now in any state that rules out his ever remembering it. They differ dispositionally. If A believes that p (in the usual dispositional sense), he will have an actual or operational (in short, not dispositional) belief that p, at the proper times — or if not at all such times, then often enough for this to be in his character. If his belief is grounded in knowledge he will (often enough) be actually aware that it is so grounded: he will be aware that he *knows* that p. This says very little, since I have not fixed what I think is to count as an actual belief or awareness, or a proper time, or how often we must do a thing to make it characteristic. On the other hand, A unquestionably lacks the disposition *freely knowing that p* if he is *never* aware of a belief that p which is grounded in knowledge that p. He also lacks it (I think) if this happens rarely or trivially enough to be called aberration. For one has to do something characteristically — that is, be disposed to it — before one can show an aberration away from it. *Not* knowing freely that p will therefore be what is in character. (From another point of view we might take such an aberration from A's usual state as evidence *for* his having *buried* knowledge that p: buried rather than lost.) 'Rarely' and 'trivially' are of course as vague here as 'often enough' or 'proper time'.

All these terms are vague, all allow degrees, and in any given case their meanings will interact. So although we may count many particular cases as clear, I think that there is no general rule which can tell us exactly when A believes that p, or what it means exactly to say that he does. Consequently we have no clear general rule for telling free from buried knowledge. One might make this complaint in a sceptical way about any dispositional term; but 'believe' remains slippery this side of scepticism.

That is why the loophole exists. For example, if I believe that you are hopelessly indiscreet, I may be expected not to tell you — though I know it would win me an argument — some fact that would embarrass me if it were widely known. Nevertheless I might. But now suppose that I tell you, for the same reason, a thing that if known would put me in jail for life: can we still reasonably hold that I believe you to be indiscreet, whatever else I may characteristically do? (Unless I want to risk jail for life; and I rule that out *ex hypothesi*.) Furthermore when I show in this way that I cannot believe you to be hopelessly indiscreet (let us call this p) am I not showing that I really believe you *not* to be so (~p)? For your discretion is too obviously at issue here to allow the other usual possibility: that I had not thought about it at all.

I would say 'no' to the first question. Since your discretion is so important here, we cannot now reasonably hold that I believe that p. But I would not always answer 'yes' to the second. Here, for example, is a thing that would in turn discredit any claim that I believe ~p (at least I think it would). Suppose that I knew another fact which would save you a good deal of pain if I told it to you, and I hate to see you in pain; but it could be dangerous to you if you did not keep it a secret. Any normally discreet person could keep it a secret without trouble unless he positively courted danger, and I know that you do not. A good time comes for telling you and *with all this in mind and for no good reason* I do not. Now in theory I could do both these things more or less at once: risk arrest by telling you Secret 1 and leave you in distress by not telling you Secret 2. This is not acting as though your discretion were in doubt. If I thought that, characteristically I would act the other way round: I would not risk telling you Secret 1 but might venture Secret 2. In short, what I do is inconsistent and puzzling, but — this is the point — most of us have met such behaviour. We have words like 'contrariness' to name it. That is the difference between 'believes' and (say) 'boils at 110° C'. It could (logically) happen that a liquid will boil today at 110° C and tomorrow, with no relevant change of conditions that anyone can find, at some other temperature; but neither our words nor our acts take serious note of this. If a liquid boils today at 110° C, and we are sure that it did, and in what conditions, we take this without a qualm as showing a fixed disposition in it to boil at that temperature in those conditions. We also take it to falsify both 'does not boil at 110° C' (in those conditions) and 'boils at a temperature other than 110° C'. We treat 'believes that p', 'does not believe that p' and 'believes that ~p' in very generally the same way, but with far less assurance. And if 'believes that p' need not always contradict either 'does not believe that p' or 'believes that ~p' and if for the same reason 'believes neither p nor ~p' need not always mean 'believes that the issue is in doubt' or 'has not thought of the issue', then the distinction between free and buried knowledge is equally uncertain, and so is the logic of 'deceive'.

My earlier arguments took it for granted that either (1) '*A believes that p*' or (2) '*A does not believe that p*' must be true (given that A exists and is a proper subject for 'believes') and that (1) and (2) cannot both be true at once; also that (2) will mean that either (2a) '*A believes that ~p*' is true, or (2b) '*A believes that he cannot tell whether p or ~p*', or (2c) '*The issue of p or ~p does not occur to A*'; and that again no two of these three can be true at once. But human contrariness may make us think that this need not be so after all. '*A believes that p, and it is false that A believes that p*' — that is (1 & ~1) — is too blatant a contradiction, and so is (2 & ~2). But '*A believes and does not believe that p*' — that is, (1 & 2) — seems not to be the same as either. I think that we would use it figuratively on the whole, to mean that A's beliefs vary or that he acts as though they do; but I suppose that we might sometimes mean it literally. If so we can only escape contradicting ourselves if we suppose that '*A does not believe that p*' says that A has a *second* disposition towards p *as well as the first* (to believe that p). It can no longer mean that he has not the first. Even so 'A believes and does not believe that p' seems to me a bad way to put it; but people have too often suggested it to me as a possible form for self-deception for me to ignore it. If my first analysis of (2) still holds, this second disposition must be (2a), (2b), (2c) or some combination of these.

'*A believes that p and also that ~p*' — that is, (1 & 2a) in as natural a form as I can think of — is not clearly a contradiction. It does not even seem to entail that A believes the clear contradiction 'p & ~p'. And if it did, I think that we could not take it seriously; for what could it be to believe that? We cannot *behave* as though something of the form 'p & ~p' were true (as opposed to behaving as though they were true in different ways, or as though 'true' were meaningless and life Absurd) because the case is inconceivable. We can say it; but to show belief we must say it with understanding and sincerity, which in this case will not mix. Denying the law of non-contradiction does not give a new way of understanding, it makes 'understand' unusable. So if A understands any statement of the form 'p & ~p' he cannot sincerely assent to it (that is if he treats it literally); and if he thinks that he assents to it, he does not understand it.

But if (1 & 2a) does not entail '*A believes that (p & ~p)*', one of two things must be true. Either A actually (that is, non-dispositionally) believes that p and that ~p at different times, or he can sometimes believe actually and at once both that p and that ~p, with no further belief that (p & ~p). The first is not a logical puzzle: (1 & 2a) would then mean that A's beliefs alternate in a peculiar way. He shows an actual belief that p often enough for anyone, in normal circumstances, not to doubt that he has this disposition; but he also, abnormally, shows an actual belief that ~p just as often at other times. My story about the two secrets could be a case of this, though I for one would not choose an expression so paradoxical-looking as (1 & 2a) if I wanted to describe it literally. (1 & 2a) may say *something* literal about belief, but it does so in a confusing way. On the other hand if we treat it as a figure of speech it suggests rather well the fact that contrary behaviour may confuse us almost as much as a paradox in logic. And this could often be enough to make us say it, without thinking whether we mean it literally or not: it feels right, never mind why.

But if this is what we mean, it is not literal self-deception. When A knows and (because he knows) is aware of a belief that p, his knowledge is free. When he is aware of a belief that ~p, his first belief has gone and his knowledge is buried. The two states do not overlap. Any stages between, when neither belief is actual, are best called not times when A believes that p and also that ~p (using dispositional terms in a way that can only confuse) but times when A is uncertain about p or is not thinking of p at all. At times like these his knowledge must be buried.

Now for the other possibility: that A can believe that p and believe that ~p, actually and at once. When 'A' names a whole individual — as it does here — this seems to depend on whether A can do two different things at the same time, each of which counts independently as actual belief. For example, if merely *acting as if* were enough to count and so was *sincere and intelligent assent* even when unspoken, A would need only to act as if ~p with a sincere mental reservation that p and the thing would be done. (But that is hypocrisy, not self-deception.) And what will count must indeed (I think) always fall somewhere in the range of: acting as if p; feeling as if p; thinking as if p (that is, imagining); thinking *that* p (that is, assenting to p). But for our purpose the range is narrower: we want only those senses of 'believe' that will identify a deliberate deceiver and his victim. This means that A must think *that* p, whatever else in the range he must do (see pages 11 to 14). So this second possibility drops out; for I do not see how A could assent at once to p and to ~p without also assenting to (p & ~p), if we suppose that the same man in all his aspects assents in each case.

(1 & 2b) seems impossible too. The statement '*p, but I can't tell whether p or ~p*' may not contradict itself formally, but it is self-stultifying: it can no more be assented to if one understands it properly than '*p & ~p*'. Since we need a sense of 'believe' that includes assent, (1 & 2b) works out rather like (1 & 2a). All it can literally mean is that A's actual beliefs vary in a peculiar way, or perhaps that he thinks that p but feels as though he did not.

(1 & 2c): 2c is not dispositional, it describes a state of affairs. I suspect that it is one that will not mix with any state at all where A actually believes that p; and when belief must include assent as it must here, (1 & 2c) is impossible.

There is one more way in which A might not believe that p. *A could be so confused about p* (2d) that this cannot be analysed into changes to and from any of the other states of belief. This disturbed or cloudy state will surely not allow intelligent assent to p, so '*1 & 2d*' too, I think, can only mean that A's condition varies when the question of p arises — this time between actual belief that p and confusion about it. And whenever A knows that p but (2d) is also true, his knowledge that p must be buried. (Combinations of (2a), (2b), (2c) and (2d) may be analysed along the same lines, but this is not immediately relevant.)

All this suggests that 'believe' and 'know' leave no loopholes after all, if we take them in the sense that we need. But if we may not use these, nor stronger words in the same range (like 'admit'), nor weaker ones (like 'accept' in some of its senses), we seem to have nothing left. Certainly the usual ways of speaking both about self- and standard deception suggest no different, unrelated family of terms that can take their place. This means that self-deception is impossible, if the whole individual is to be at once deceiver and deceived.

Before I go on, I want to say something more about the idea of buried knowledge. Why do I mention only knowledge? Why not also buried belief? For certainly by analogy with buried knowledge we could if we liked speak of buried belief. But *when we mean 'belief' in the epistemological sense, and when 'A' stands for the whole individual* I think it is misleading.

Buried belief, by analogy with buried knowledge, would occur when A at first freely believes that p; then does not, and perhaps even freely believes that ~p; then does again, in some way that makes it sensible to say that in spite of appearances, A believed that p all the time. This means that something must be true about A in the middle stage which, in spite of appearances, in itself amounts to belief. But if we mean something that A forgets and later remembers, that is buried *knowledge*: of p's content, or that he used to believe that p, or his former reasons for believing it, or things that he might now take to be a reason — any or all of these. And he could know things like this, even freely, as he does when he remembers them, and still not quite believe that p. At most they are reasons for believing, not belief itself. The only exception will be when what he remembers is *knowing* that p.

In short, he must also *assent* to p again the second time round. If he does not, the status of his belief that p is not in question: it has been lost. He may of course have had in the middle stage a temperamental predisposition to assent to p in some situations, perhaps just those situations where he openly knows p's content, his former reasons, and so on; but again this predisposition is not a belief that p. He could have it all his life and never believe that p, if the situation never holds. In short, what exists in the middle stage is a set of conditions for belief that p — things either buried (A's knowledge) or latent (A's predisposition to assent) — with one necessary condition missing.

And in fact where buried belief seems most plausible we do *not* mean the kind of thing that I have described; or so I think. We mean something like this: A claims not to believe that p in the epistemological sense, but in some ways it looks as if he does. He may show (or seem to show) emotions for example that are unrealistic unless p is true. Such behaviour may be only hypocrisy, as we have seen. We begin to think of buried beliefs instead, if we also see contrariness in A. Typically he will act in other ways as though he does *not* believe that p, or believes that ~p — enough so that, other things being equal, his disbelief would seem to be real.

But behaviour, whether it matches one's epistemological beliefs or belies them, is never buried. What seems to be buried here is (once again) knowledge: A seems oddly never to be *aware of the fact* that *he very often acts as if p, in spite of his professed disbelief.* To posit buried belief here as well as buried knowledge is to go beyond behaviour to the interpretation of behaviour. We may feel that only one thing can explain A's contrariness: somehow he must after all believe that p in the epistemological sense; but the belief is out of reach, 'in a corner of his mind'. But this is to treat A's mind, and therefore A, as split. We should therefore save 'buried belief' for that context. So long as we are trying to use 'A' for the whole man, it has no place, for I hope that I have shown how it leads to paradox here if we say that A both believes that p and does not.

Though self-deception seems impossible in an undivided A, we still have the second option. A bites himself for example if and only if one part of A bites another. We might in the same way be able to distinguish parts or aspects of A (A₁ and A₂) such that one can deceive the other, as (whole) A would deceive (whole) B. But my account of deception will rule out most of the distinctions that we might think of first. A₁ and A₂ cannot, for instance, be two parts of A's body, nor body *versus* mind, because both must have mental attributes. Since these mental attributes are also epistemological (knowing, believing, being kept from knowing or made to believe), A₁ and A₂ cannot be A's understanding *versus* his emotions. Nor do I think that they can be conscious *versus* unconscious A, in any strict sense of 'unconscious' — although there is obviously much more to say about the role(s) that an unconscious mind can play in self-deception. I shall come back to it later. What matters here is that if we are to take 'deceive' literally, both A₁ and A₂ must, it seems, be able to be aware of things. The deceiver must freely know; his victim must either be kept from knowing freely or must be led to believe. He must therefore be capable of knowing freely and of believing, in too strong a sense of 'believe' to leave out consciousness.

There is of course the loophole that I mentioned before: A₁ and A₂ might be A at different stages. Common usage might have allowed me to include this in my earlier discussion, since though names usually name whole people, this need not mean the person at every stage of his life. But in fact it amounts to two aspects of A that are distinct, so the idea belongs here. It seems rather farfetched, but I think that it is worth discussing.

If A_1 and A_2 are A at two different stages, they cannot both exist at once; but then there is no time during which a deception could take place. If A_1 deceives A_2 it can only be at an instant. It is true that we normally speak of self-deception as though it endured in time; but we might instead be referring to a series of distinct events, each one of a peculiar kind. They would take this form. Let T_1 and T_2 be two periods in A's life, ending and beginning respectively at a certain instant t. At all times in T_1 A knows that p, openly; at all times in T_2 A's knowledge that p is either buried or lost; and A himself deliberately causes or helps to cause the change.

Instant deception as such is not unthinkable. Someone who knows that p might fake a piece of 'evidence' for $\sim$p or against p which could be taken in at a glance; someone else might fall for it the instant that he sees it. We should probably think in terms of a very short but not timeless 'specious present' during which he takes it in. If so we could make this fit self-deception by saying that t divides A's life during T_1 from that 'specious present'. But the deceiver knows that the 'evidence' is a fake, and the victim, if he falls for it, can know neither this, nor that the deceiver meant it to fool him. So when A_1 is A-in-T_1 and A_2 is A-in-T_2, A must arrange among other things to lose his memory of the faking, either before t or at it. In theory he could do it, by self-hypnosis or perhaps a drug, and some self-deceptive manoeuvres seem not unlike this. ('Why do you drink?' — 'To forget.' — 'To forget what?' — 'That I drink.') But most do not; and even those that do are not like enough. They lack just what makes this schema (in theory) work: an A_1 with unusual skills or fantastically selective memory drugs. For if A_2 is to be successfully deceived, he must be left with no idea that his views on the subject have been tampered with — unless he cares so little about it that it is not a likely topic for self-deception. Instant self-deception then is clearly not the answer.

If no other candidates for A_1 and A_2 seem immediately obvious, we might be tempted to define them *ad hoc* ('Let A_1 be the deceiver . . .'). But this is to beg the question of whether such a division is possible, that is, whether self-deception literally is possible. Nor can we look for help to other terms like 'discipline' or 'criticism', whose first use is non-reflexive and whose literal reflexive uses ('self-discipline', etc.) seem to demand the same division. They might demand much the same kind, but not exactly the same. Moreover, even if the logic of these terms, whatever it is, is exactly the same in this respect, this may simply mean that their reflexive use happens always to be metaphor. We cannot know that this is not so, unless we already know that the A_1 and A_2 in terms of which we analyse them are real distinct aspects of A.

For much the same reason we cannot appeal to a model — as Plato, for example, used a city to argue for a rather different division of the self. Any model or analogy is open to this objection. As long as it is a model and not the thing itself it will be unlike the thing itself in some way or other, and perhaps at just the point in question. We can know that this is not so only when we already know what both are like in this respect; but if we know what *both* are like, we do not need the model. This is not to say that models are not useful heuristically; but they prove nothing.

The logic of words and concepts — 'deceive', 'believe' and so forth — can take us no further. If we want to find an appropriate A_1 and A_2 (or to decide what 'self-deception' stands for if there are none), we need facts.

3   SELVES THAT CAN DECEIVE EACH OTHER

ACCORDING to my schema in Chapter 2, a deceiver must know something that his victim does not know. More exactly, he must both know and believe something that his victim may know, but cannot also believe. This seems to demand two people; but for one kind of human being this need not be so. The various 'selves' of an individual with multiple (or dissociated) personality seem often to be enough like separate people to make it work, as my examples will show. (See Appendix A on sources for this chapter.) If this in any way counts as self-deception, we must not expect it to be the normal kind — if there is a normal kind; but I think it sheds light from an unusual angle, in a way that will be useful later on.

Multiple personality may exist when there is no dissociation of memory or consciousness: the individual simply shifts between two or more different characters. Typically each will speak of the others in the third person, and will not allow that they are in any way himself; but each will know anything that the others can remember. Example 2 (below) is a case of this kind. A personality that remembers another's experiences may however insist with good evidence that this is not just because he has access to the other's memories. He is conscious of the other's experiences as they happen, as a spectator. (See Example 3.) On the other hand, one personality may have no memory of the other at all, nor any present awareness; he may not even know that the other exists.

A simple case of this last kind would be two personalities that alternate with no memory of each other, so that neither can know the other directly: Mary Reynolds for example. She is discussed by William McDougall[11] at some length and by W.S. Taylor and M.F. Martin in their survey article on multiple personality.[12] Hers is thought to be the first published case. This seems no reason to doubt her credentials however. I choose her because she is a straightforward example of a common feature. Personalities that alternate with some amnesia are found in 59 cases out of Taylor and Martin's 76; 40 of these include pairs whose amnesia works both ways.

(Example 1) [Mary Reynolds] was considered normal until she was about eighteen. Then she began to have occasional 'fits' which were evidently hysterical. Some months after a severe one she slept eighteen or twenty hours, and awoke seeming to know scarcely anything she had learned. She soon became acquainted with her surroundings, however, and within a few weeks learned reading, calculating, and writing, though her penmanship was crude compared to what it had been.

. . .After five weeks of this new life, she slept long again, and awoke as her 'normal' self, with no memory for what she had experienced since her recent lapse. Thereafter the 'new' or 'second state' and the 'old' or 'first state', as she came to call them, alternated irregularly. The second state gained over the first, however, and became more rich and subtle, until the woman was about thirty-six years old. At that time the second state became permanent and continued until her death in 1854.[13]

MR1 was 'melancholy, shy and given to solitary religious meditations', MR2 was 'buoyant, witty, fond of company and a lover of nature'. McDougall's longer account adds that in the second state her amnesia of the first state was not always complete.

In this late period *she sometimes seemed to have dim dreamlike* memories of her life in the primary state. And once, when in this second state, *she dreamed of a sister who had died before the second state appeared*; the sister so dreamed of was identified by her relatives from her description.[14]

(His italics, marking what he considered to be 'of special theoretical interest'.)

One can imagine MR1 finding out some family secret (p) and deciding that MR2 must not know — one cannot trust her to be discreet. Suppose that MR1 therefore destroyed all the evidence, and so kept MR2 from knowing that p, or faked 'evidence' to the contrary, so that MR1 found it and decided that ~p. MR2 and MR1 are in a sense the same person, Mary Reynolds, so this would be self-deception of a kind. It need not be instantaneous; in other ways it would work like the 'instant self-deception' of Chapter 2. But in this case the deceiver need not contrive any loss of memory at or before a given moment: she would set out to deceive her (other) self precisely because she knew the loss of memory would come.

Though this is self-deception of a kind, it need not be an interesting kind. Compare a case where I say detachedly 'How dreadful!' of something I did when I was four. This is self-criticism of a kind; but the criticised self is too far from the critic in character and responsibilities for 'self-criticism' to apply in anything but a trivial (and eccentric) way. We must examine *how* MR_1 and MR_2 are the same. If their 'self'-deception works only because they are like two people at the crux — where normal self-deceivers are not — they cannot help us.

They share a body. In fact without this (one) body we could not identify them as MR_1 and MR_2 (see the argument to this effect by Bernard Williams[15]). It can be applied to Mary Reynolds like this. Suppose that someone else (Jane Smith) has a second personality JS_2, which appears always and only when Mary Reynolds is MR_1. JS_2 has the temperament *and memory* of MR_2, and she claims to *be* MR_2 — a personality that changes bodies. She cannot prove her claim. Without the criterion of a body we have no way in which we can tell identity from mere similarity. JS_2's access to MR_2's memories is hard to explain if we say that they are not the same, only alike; but if we said that they were the same, it would be just as hard to explain how MR_2 changed bodies.

Since they share a body, neither of Mary Reynolds' two selves can deceive the other in a way that needs two bodies, by impersonating someone for example; and since they alternate in time, neither can deceive the other when both must be conscious at once. But deception between whole people may at times have special limits too — for example we cannot deceive a blind man visually — so not all such limits make real self-deception impossible. What matters is how MR_1 and MR_2 would deal with what I have argued are the main things in deception: knowledge, belief, and the way that these are caused or prevented.

(1) *Knowledge*. As MR_1 Mary Reynolds would know that p, while as MR_2 (it seems) she would not. But this ignorance would regularly turn to knowledge again without Mary Reynolds' having to re-learn that p: once again she would remember. So if we say that she was the same person all the time, we must also say that Mary Reynolds knows all along that p. This is no problem, since we need only say that when she is

MR$_2$ the knowledge is buried. We need buried knowledge anyway to explain MR$_2$, unless we want to claim that her dream and her dim memories of the first stage were clairvoyance or coincidence. In some cases of multiple personality the separate selves integrate at last into one, who has all their memories. Here buried knowledge is even more clearly needed to make sense of it all.[16]

(2) *Belief*. As MR$_1$ she would believe that p. As MR$_2$ she would not, and, depending on the form that the deception took, she might even believe that ~p. This again need not stop us from treating her as one person: we may lose and regain a belief many times. Usually, though perhaps not always, this reflects some change in our state of knowledge — which is also the case here. The alternating states that I described in (1) account well enough for Mary Reynolds' shifts in belief. But other things make her special where (1) and (2) do not.

(3) *Concealing facts* and (4) *Causing false beliefs*. Recurring (and selective) amnesia makes Mary Reynolds two people here, not one. MR$_1$ need only destroy evidence or fake it: she would never need to suppress or change her own thoughts in order to deceive MR$_2$. And yet she would know that they contradict what MR$_2$ must be made to think.

(5) *Responsibility* for (3) and (4). As MR$_1$ Mary Reynolds would act with full knowledge and from choice. This makes her responsible for the deception. As MR$_2$ she would know nothing about it, and would therefore be entirely innocent.

I conclude that we must treat Mary Reynolds as two people in some important ways and as one person in others. Where the content of her knowledge is concerned we must think of her as one, or we cannot explain MR$_2$'s 'dim dreamlike memories' of being MR$_1$; and if MR$_2$ could reach *some* of MR$_1$'s knowledge like this, nothing seems *a priori* to rule out her recalling things learned by MR$_2$. We may also think of her as one where the content of her beliefs is concerned, since she never seems to have held incompatible beliefs at once. But the way in which she buried and remembered that knowledge and changed those beliefs does not allow us to think of her as one; and so we cannot call it a self-deception in any normal sense, when one such self deceives another. It would be like saying 'He's talking to himself' about conversation between the heads of a two-headed man.

We should therefore not be surprised when those moral or half-moral terms which we associate with self-deceivers do not fit Mary Reynolds. If she deceives her (other) self in this way she is not *foolish* or *escapist* or *blind* or *wishful-thinking* or *perverse*. As MR₂ she can have no reason to believe that p, so how can we disparage her if she does not? And as MR₁ she keeps p secret in a thoroughly practical way. We might blame her for it, but only as we would blame her if she deceived another person: for dishonesty. In short, we have here an A₁ and A₂ too independent of each other to suit us.

We are likelier to use 'blind' and so forth of Dr. Morton Prince's 'BCA'[17] in her third and fourth phases. C was the original, and finally the reintegrated, personality. She was a woman with a strong sense of duty, whose life demanded self-sacrifice. A rebellious side (the 'B complex') split off and took over from C as a distinct personality.

(Example 2) During this month all the serious side of C's character, with which the B complex had so long conflicted, was in abeyance . . .. She could remember all her former life; but such recollections did not revive their usual emotional tones. She was so changed emotionally that she felt herself to be a personality distinct from her former self, C, and could not acknowledge the major experiences of her life as her own. She asserted of her son: 'He is not my son — I was never married. I know all her (C's) experiences, but they are her experiences, not mine'. And she behaved accordingly, repudiating all responsibility for her son. On the other hand, she acknowledged as her own all the thoughts and feelings which had in the past arisen from the B complex . . . [C's serious side, the 'A complex' now reappeared, first joined with B so that the whole C was there, but later alone as a separate personality. After this] for several months, these two phases [A and B] alternated frequently. There was alternation of the two personalities without amnesia on the part of either.[18]

(In BCA's fifth phase, A became amnesic of B, while B became 'intra-conscious' of A: she was aware of A's thoughts as a spectator, while A was dominant.)

B's theory that the child of her own body was not her son could easily be called foolish, perverse, blind and so forth. It would also seem nearly right to say to BCA 'You deceive yourself if you think he is not your child'. 'Delude yourself' no doubt is better, given the strangeness of the idea, but that is a question of degree. Suppose this is a real self-deception then: how would it work?

Something made BCA, in her B phase, no longer believe the

true proposition that this was her son. If that was due to deception, B was the deception's victim. If it was *self*-deception, some part of BCA deceived B, but which?

It was not A, because (1) A split off as a separate personality later than B did; (2) B knew A's memories at all times, so that A could not know any proposition and keep it from B; and finally, (3) unlike MR₁ in my story, A had no motive to deceive. The A complex was C's dutiful side, and this seems to have been the character kept by the dissociated A. It distressed and bewildered A that B should exist at all. She might well have tried to suppress or destroy B if she could; but the one thing it seems impossible for her to have wanted was to abet B in her irresponsible ways, by giving her false beliefs that excused them.

Nor was it B herself, even though B is that side of BCA which did want to free B from C's responsibilities. If we say that B deceived B we rewrite the paradoxes of Chapter 2 in miniature.

Finally there is C, the original personality before the split. C had no motive (so far as one can tell) for giving her dissociated B complex a false idea about her son. On the other hand, she had one for dissociating the B complex: the strain of a clash between A-feelings and B-feelings. It is however very unlikely that C knew splits like this were possible, far less how to cause one. And even if she did cause it somehow, this does not look at first sight like what we want: the *deception* of one part of herself by another. It is a move by a whole self to bring a dissociated 'splinter' into being.

Suppose however, for a moment, that C was responsible for the split. One main feature of B was her repudiation of C's child on the grounds that he was not also B's. If B really believed this, could we not say that C had deceived her about it?

If this exactly described the case, we should. Here is a parallel story about whole people. An ugly magician creates a beautiful girl, and gives her the belief that he is the handsomest man in the world. Has he deceived her? Of course; his ways are unusual, but still he knows a certain proposition p (that he is ugly) and makes her believe that ~p. This will fit BCA however only if B lost C's memories when she split off, and she did not. Suppose the magician had to give the girl access to his own memory: she would then know that he had at some time learned that p, had later often confirmed it, and so on. So she would know that p. She could avoid this only by doubting the magician's memory or good judgment. ('It's just that he lacks self-confidence — he's not at all ugly really. In fact . . .') But if this is her own idea, the magician did not deceive her into it; and if it was a thing that he believed himself while also knowing that p, it was not *deliberate* deception (see the types discussed in Chapter 2). And if he did not believe it, but had done something to make the girl do so, his memories would tell her not only that p was false but also how and why he had tried to fool her. So the plot could not hope to succeed — unless by 'believes that ~p' we mean only that she feels compelled to behave as if ~p, *feels* as if ~p, or in some other way falls short of epistemological belief. Or she might take another way, depending on how we interpret p. If we take 'ugly' and so forth to be purely aesthetic terms (as opposed to the way we normally take them in contexts like these) she might just have a taste in male looks which she knows to be eccentric, and which she knows that the magician made her have.

In the same way B might have felt compelled to act as though C's child were not hers, say that he was not, and so on, and yet know that really he was. Or if we take 'hers' to mean 'her responsibility', we have a moral parallel to the girl's aesthetic judgment: B might have been claiming quite sincerely that she felt bound by an eccentric moral intuition which she knew that C had made her have and C did not share. What seems impossible is that C could have kept B from knowing that the child also was biologically B's. If B remembered C's knowing it, B would know it — unless she was too cloudy-minded or stupid to interpret C's memories correctly, and there is no evidence for that at all. B would also have been able to explain — like the magician's girl — why she felt compelled as she did; so although C compelled her, C could not deceive her.

Of course the records of the case might be wrong. C might have had some memories that B never reached, and B might not have known this. C could have deceived B at least about *their* contents by making B split off. This would be even more like the 'instant self-deception' of Chapter 2 than the Mary Reynolds story, and correspondingly less like any ordinary kind.

In any case the parallel with my magician story is nearly

incredible. C would have had deliberately to create B as a separate personality, by dissociating one aspect of herself. Multiple personality is very rare, and in C's day discussion of it seems to have been kept to the technical books and journals. C seems to have had no experience or interest (before her own split) in anything of the kind. Every report suggests that the split came quite without warning. Strain was no doubt a source of it somehow; but it was in no way an act to be rid of strain.

And yet BCA, who by this account did *not* deceive herself literally, is more what we expect self-deceivers to be like than Mary Reynolds. Why?

Assume that the split was not meant or foreseen. (I think that we must.) We now have what looks like a familiar paradox. However it happened, B claimed to believe that C's child was not hers; but both C and A knew that he was, and B could remember anything that they could. How *can* she really have thought as she claimed? This is also a question we ask about self-deceivers in general: how *can* they believe something contrary to what they must know?

In B's case the answer seems to be this. If B thought that C's son was not born from the body that was also B's, she cannot after all have shared C's (*free*) knowledge, or A's. She must have become deluded — a commonplace compared to multiple personality. But this does not seem to have been what she meant by 'He is her son, not mine'. Her point was that when the child was produced, the body was under different management.

She seems to have argued along these lines. (1) when C chose to marry, one element in her was against it and would have rebelled if it could. This was the B complex. It had no part in any act that led to C's marriage. So (2) it had no part in the marriage. (3) This B complex later split off to become B. So (4) B had no part in C's marriage, that is, it was not B's marriage. (5) C's son was the child of this marriage. So (6) C's son was not B's child.

Before B split off, C could not have thought of points (3), (4) and (6): they are about B. C cannot then have known that they were false; and C knew that (5) was not false, but true. Later B split off and C knew it; and A always knew it, because A split off after B. But it is not clear that even at that stage C or A could prove B wrong on any point of knowledge. (1) and (3) are theory, and in any case C and A seem to have held that theory too. They disputed (4), (6) and probably (2). But these are not pure matters of fact, they involve interpretation.

(2) and (4) disagree with the (United States) marriage law, as this is normally interpreted. A marriage is supposed to bind the whole individual. But B did not have to deny this, only to say that she was a special case whom the law did not fit. One clear reason why the law can be taken to bind whole individuals must be that multiple personality is so rare. For a marriage requires the full consent of both parties; and if one of them has several selves who cannot agree, the question of full consent becomes complicated to say the least. A and C certainly disagreed with B on this point, but it was a disagreement in judgment, where other judgments could be made. B might for example have got support from the lawyer of Evelyn Lancaster (Example 3 below) who thought it safer, all things considered, if both Eve Black and Eve White signed Evelyn's will.[19]

(6) is more obviously eccentric. B's point about consent is relevant to marriage, but we would surely call a boy a woman's son if her body conceived and bore him — no more is needed. Of course nobody can normally be both the child of his mother's marriage and the child of a mother who never married; but then by normal standards B was married: she could not appeal to that to support her on point (6). It comes to this: B (abnormally) had to choose between '*child of C's body, and mine*' and '*child of C's marriage but not of mine*'. Surely, other things being equal, the first outranks the second. B claimed that other things were not equal because 'she was changed so emotionally': she could not *feel* that a child was hers whom 'someone else' had taken the steps to have. But even a raped woman's child is her child, even if she hates it. Feeling is not the main issue.

B must have known that people would find her claim unreasonable, and her arguments sophistry. But she does not seem strictly to have contradicted any fact that she or A or the whole C ever knew; and that seems to be what let her claim it. And this I think is a thing she shares with those we more typically call self-deceivers: they may be untiringly subtle when it comes to logic, while ignoring the usual standards of what is reasonable. (I am not saying that this is all they do, or even that they all do this; only that it is very common.) If so, self-deceivers seem to be like BCA in how they *avoid* literally deceiving themselves: an interesting conclusion.

I have said that in some alternating personalities only one of a pair will remember both stages, while the other is amnesic of its partner. (This became true of BCA in her fifth stage.) A simple case of this one-way access or one-way amnesia could add no possibilities for self-deception to those of my Examples 1 and 2. The remembering self could deceive the other as MR_1 could have deceived MR_2 and *vice versa;* the amnesic could no more deceive the remembering self than BCA's A could have deceived B. So I shall not discuss a simple case; my third example mixes one-way access to the other self's memory with a new feature, *intraconsciousness*: one personality knows the other's thoughts as they occur, while that other is dominant. This means that both are sometimes conscious at once. (Co-consciousness turns up in 23 cases out of Taylor and Martin's 76, intraconsciousness in 8.)

(Example 3) Some twenty-five years ago Drs C.H. Thigpen and H. Cleckley published a report on a patient whom they called 'Eve White'; her full name they later represented by the pseudonym 'Evelyn Lancaster'.[20] Later they wrote a popularising book, *The Three Faces of Eve*,[21] which gives more detail and more documentary material — letters, entries in a diary, medical reports. Apart from these we should be wary of accepting it: according to 'Eve' herself it is in many ways wrong, and so is a sequel, *The Final Face of Eve*.[22] She has now published an autobiography[23] under her real name. According to this she had (for example) many more personalities than three, and their 'integration' at the book's end was by no means final. (See Appendix A.) Her different personalities, however, seem always to have followed the same pattern of memory and consciousness as those in Thigpen and Cleckley's first report and in *The Three Faces of Eve:* a concentric one. Personality A is intraconscious of Personality B but not *vice versa*; Personality C is intraconscious of B and A, but neither is aware of her — and so on. And about the early stages of the case, those dealing with the two personalities 'Eve White' and 'Eve Black', the real 'Eve' (Chris Costner Sizemore) and her doctor/journalists tell the same story. I shall therefore concentrate on that.

Eve White complained of 'blackouts'. There were times during which — according to other people — she was conscious, but of which she herself remembered nothing. She also could not explain uncharacteristic things that other people claimed she had done; and once or twice she had heard a voice that she knew was not real. She was afraid that she was going mad. This in itself (Dr Thigpen says) was surprising: to hear voices is typically a symptom of 'grave mental disturbance', but to recognize them as such is anything but typical: she was reacting to signs of madness in a way that was perfectly sane. Then one day in the doctor's office an alternating personality appeared: 'Eve Black'. EW knew nothing of EB: when EB took over, she 'blacked out'. But EB claimed that she had existed ever since EW was a child, and was able to explain certain things that the child EW had never understood, mainly punishments for things that EW was sure that she had not done. EB could remember anything that EW could; she also stayed awake when EW was dominant or 'out' and EB was 'in': *I know her thoughts like she knows them herself. I don't think 'em, of course. But I can nearly always tell whatever's on her mind.'*[24]

She distinguished EW's thoughts from her own clearly and without sympathy. She could also, she said, ignore them and think about something else if they bored her. EB's way with EW is in all this very like 'Sally's' to the famous Miss Beauchamp's personality 'B₁' (the 'saint');[25] Sally seems however only to have come out completely when Miss Beauchamp was hypnotized. But it seems that she could, while co-conscious, force B₁ to do things that embarrassed or distressed her, like suddenly winding her knitting wool round all the furniture. EB does not seem to have done things like this to EW, though she claimed once to have stopped EW from killing herself by forcing herself 'out' in EW's place.[26] And

Even while invisible and inaudible [Eve Black], apparently, has means of disturbing Eve White. . . . She explains that the hallucinatory or quasi-hallucinatory voice which Eve White heard before the other Eve disclosed herself was her deliberate work. . . . She furthermore insists that she can, with considerable effort, often 'pick out' or erase from Eve White's reach certain items of memory. 'I just start thinking about it very hard.' Eve Black says 'and after a while she quits and it doesn't come back to her anymore'. . . . Such a claim, obviously, was subject to testing by the therapist. Several experiments indicated that it was correct.[27]

This passage suggests that EB could deceive EW in all the ways open to a personality whose victim was amnesic of her (like MR₁ and MR₂) and in other ways as well. She could speak to EW directly as a 'quasi-hallucinatory' voice; and since EW never knew EB's thoughts, this means that EB could in theory have told EW lies. She could also erase EW's memories some- times by 'picking them out', or more exactly — since nothing seems *a priori* to have ruled out EW's eventually recalling them — EB could bury them. EW on the other hand could not deceive EB in any way: *'I know her thoughts like she knows them herself'*. In short, EW was transparent to EB as one is supposed to be only to oneself, but EB was opaque to EW as one person is to someone else. And though EW was transparent to EB this does not make them, when EW was awake, into a normal person. 'Picking out' a thought for example takes two streams of consciousness, not one — even though both may be trans- parent to the picker, and to some extent in the picker's control.

All this makes the case histories of Eve and her kind required study for anyone who offers a general theory of consciousness, or pretends to assess other people's theories; and so *a fortiori* for students of self-deception, or so it seems to me. I shall come back to her many times. It also makes her even less a 'normal' self-deceiver than Mary Reynolds. I said in Chapter 2 that an individual's knowledge cannot at once be both buried and not buried; this is true of Mary Reynolds but not of Evelyn Lan- caster. I think we must say that she is not by the usual standards an individual: she lacks too many things which that concept takes for granted. There is only one important way in which she is one person as regards knowledge, and not two people or a freak with extraordinary features: it is that EW at least was transparent to Eve as a whole. EW was also, we may note, the side that could *not* deceive her (other) self.

All this applies *a fortiori* to the only basic type of multiple personality which I have not discussed: two or more co- conscious selves which are all transparent to each other. To sum up: literal deception *can* sometimes take place in a single human being; and it can work in ways that we do not find when separate human beings deceive each other: for example, EB making EW forget things simply by thinking about them very hard herself. But this only happens when the deceiver's thoughts are out of the victim's reach — a thing that we do not expect in ordinary people who have one personality apiece.

The way we speak of multiple personality reflects this. I think that 'self' has a clear literal use when it is reflexive: for any relation R, 'A has R to himself' means 'A has R to A'. As soon as we treat 'self' as a noun, its literal meaning becomes uncertain. I am not even sure that it has any, except where it stands apart as a noun but still works reflexively. 'To thine own self be true' for example seems to say the same thing as 'Be true to thyself'. At any rate when we speak of somebody's *having* more than one self, this is quite clearly metaphorical; and that is what we say of people like Eve. When one such self deceives another, then, this is still not literal self-deception: while 'deceive' can be literal, 'self' becomes a metaphor.

4 PHILONOUS AND HYLAS ON DISSOCIATION

I shall come back to my multiple personality examples at many points. They give us evidence of what is possible. In particular they give counter-examples to certain theories about the mind which (in turn) have led to theories about self-deception. But they do seem on the face of it very different from the usual run of people: a split that leads to separate 'selves' also produces deception that looks more interpersonal than reflexive. We need something more like the split in 'A bites himself', where A bites one part of himself with another, but it still seems right to say that subject and object both are A. Since we do not credit ordinary people with more than one 'self', any split that we can find in *them* may allow this — provided that it is also a split which allows deception of any kind at all. Common usage (as I explored it in Chapter 2) is no help when it comes to deciding whether any such split is possible: it gives us the term 'self-deception' with one hand and an analysis leading to paradox with the other. But why hope for more from common usage, which grows up anyhow, and can shape a concept impartially out of observation, prejudice, convenience and fossilized myth? People may be quite unlike what it suggests.

In multiple personality what allows either deception (EB/EW) or something more like ordinary *self*-deception (BCA) is *dissociation* of some kind: a split between some of the individual's thinking and the rest, so that they do not work together in the usual way. A first step could therefore be to look for parallels in the rest of us and then, if we find any, to ask if they go with self-deceptive behaviour.

Hypnosis can cause such splits. It is artificial; but it seems to work on most people to some extent, not just on people with several personalities. Through hypnosis people can be made to forget long periods when they were conscious, and later to remember again, as did Mary Reynolds for example. Or take this (quite standard) example of post-hypnotic suggestion:

(Example 4) I tell B, during hypnosis, that when I put my hand in my pocket he will open the window. After he has wakened and opened the window, I ask him why he did so. If B is not amnesic for the hypnotic period, he will probably say: 'Because you told me to do so'. But if he is amnesic he will give some plausible reason, e.g. although the air may be cool and fresh, he may say the room seemed to him stuffy and hot. . . . In such cases, if one allows the post-hypnotic action to pass without remark, and a little later inquires about it, B will deny all memory of the action. . . . Now suppose we complicate the situation and tell B that he will open the window when I put my hand in my pocket for the ninth time. I waken B and engage him in conversation, putting my hand in and out of my pocket occasionally, and he carries out the suggestion. If B is closely observed, it may be noticed that he seems to keep a furtive watch on my hands. Yet if, either before or after carrying out the suggestion, I ask him whether he is aware of any suggestion I have given him for post-hypnotic action, he will stoutly deny all knowledge of instruction.[28]

If someone asks B why he opened the window, he rationalizes; if nobody speaks of it he seems to forget that he did it. Here even more than with BCA I think we have behaviour that looks like 'natural' self-deception. Mr D for example has just poured himself another whisky when his wife looks in to call him to lunch.

'You always say you only drink in the evening!'

'What? Oh well, so I do normally. You know that. As a matter of fact I think I may be getting a cold today — thought I needed something to keep me going.'

'You must feel coldy most of the time, then. Every time I look in these days you've got a glass in your hand.'

'What? NONSENSE. You're exaggerating quite absurdly, woman. Anybody who knows me will tell you . . .' — and so on, and so forth; and D really seems not to remember how often he has been drinking during the day when his wife came in, but made no comment — not to mention the glasses that he has poured himself when no one was there to see.

If D's behaviour is not only coincidentally like B's, Example 4 may tell us something about it. For B, unlike D, has no reason to lie; and B's behaviour, unlike D's, is artifically brought about. We therefore know a little better what is going on. One thing that it usefully confirms is that *a loss of memory like this can happen*, however little we may want (in D's case) to concede it. And there is more that we can say about B, and therefore perhaps about D as well.

The nine hand-in-pockets are taken account of: they must be, since B carries out the suggestion. But B does not know this, or so it seems; at least it does not look like open knowledge. We may therefore decide that it takes no conscious thought at all — a well-known alternative to which I shall come back. But we need not. B-after-waking (call him 'BW') is amnesic of the experiences of B-when-hypnotized ('BH'), although other cases show that he could get the memory back through re-hypnosis. In short, hypnosis makes B look like a one-shot Mary Reynolds. But BH does not lapse entirely when BW takes over, for something unknown to BW still leads B to act, on instructions that were given to BH. This *might* be taken to suggest that BH is less like a simple alternating personality (Mary Reynolds) than like one who stays awake while the other is dominant, awake and active enough at least to make B shut the window 'automatically' at a signal, in other words to do a thing that the dominant B neither meant to do nor foresaw.

When Miss Beauchamp's dominant B_1 found (to her dismay) that she had wound her wool round all the furniture, it turned out that the intra-conscious Sally had made her do it — or so Sally claimed, when brought out and given a chance to talk. So here at least, when we can learn about an automatic act as it were from inside, we find a fully (intra-)conscious and deliberate agent — or so it seems. This suggests that it is possible in theory that the aspect of B which is continuous with BH and which leads B to open the window may also work intra-consciously and deliberately. McDougall (from whom I take the example) seems to have a theory of this kind; and since it is one which allows an 'A_1' that can literally deceive, we must consider it seriously. (From now on I shall call the conscious or unconscious extension of BH that leads B to open the window 'Bx', and the combination BH + Bx I shall call 'BHx'.)

As we recall Sally Beauchamp, we might also recall Eve Black. It seems that she could bury Eve White's knowledge by taking it to herself: 'I just start thinking about it very hard . . .'; Example 4 might in theory work the same way. BW forgets that he has opened the window unless he is made to think about it at the time. If BHx (while keeping track of the hands and carrying the suggestion out) is somehow concentrating on it, this could be where the memory is buried: BHx might take it over as a matter of course. Eve Black (so far as I know) never says how she first found out the trick of making Eve White forget, but the likeliest explanation is surely that at first it happened spontaneously, and she noticed it.

Our 'natural' self-deceiver D has if anything a slightly better chance than B to be like Eve White in this way. Even if Bx did work intra-consciously, it could not be for very long. There would almost certainly not be time for BHx to find out how to make BW forget, even if this were possible. Moreover we cannot credit BHx with anything like a motive for making BW forget that he shut the window, or (more neutrally) credit B with such a motive. The hypnotist tells him only that he will forget the instruction, not the act. But self-deceivers, we usually think, do have a motive: to avoid some unpleasant truth. D's unpleasant truth is that he drinks too much — other things too perhaps, but at any rate that. He may also have been trying not to face it for a long time; so if D had a dissociated but intra-conscious gremlin (Dx) at work, Dx might have time to learn how to make D forget things. Let me stress that I am not saying this is what happens, but only that in theory it could.

In Example 4, B's behaviour is due to the hypnotist who (1) contrives to dissociate BHx from BW (this is true whether Bx is conscious or not) and so (2) gets B to carry out a suggestion that BW knows nothing about. It involves 'a furtive watch' of the hypnotist's hands, and counting. What evidence have we that the same kind of thing might happen spontaneously?

Taking (1) first: short amnesias are common enough, for various reasons. Dr X for instance is wakened at three in the morning by the telephone: a patient wanting advice. He holds a long, clear-headed conversation which the patient later remembers; but he cannot himself remember anything about it next day or ever after. Mr Y finds himself in the spare bedroom with a pot of glue in his hand and no idea what he meant to do with it; and so forth. These lapses may be combined with (apparently) automatic action: I have heard from actors for example that it is not uncommon, in a play that has had a long run, to wake up to yourself suddenly onstage halfway through Act III and realize that you have been playing your part on automatic pilot while you were mentally redecorating your house. And then (2): this is exactly how someone like D may pour himself another glass at dinner, and another. He seems engrossed in the talk, but the corner of his eye is always on the bottle: when his hand goes out to it absentmindedly, it never misses.

X's telephone call comes between two phases of sleep and this seems to be what makes him forget it: such things are common. The actor's part in the play has become routine. But lapses — or apparent lapses — like D's are common enough too, and need explaining. They look too much like B's, I suggest, for us to ignore the likeness; and in B's case (1) and (2) come from the hypnotist's instructions, which B somehow takes account of. There seems no reason on the face of it why some corresponding program for action should not lead to a lot that D does: the program in this case coming from within D. (Again this will be true whether Dx works consciously or not.) Some dissociations in short, like Dr X's, do not need explaining in terms of motive or program or function; others like B's *and D's* make no sense without one, that is, if D really dissociates (forgets, fails to notice) as I here suggest. At any rate he acts as though he does, and because of B we know that such things are possible.

Here too we have a parallel in multiple personality, that most extreme form of dissociation. One common cause of lost memory is a knock on the head — in which case the loss is clearly in no way 'motivated' — and at least once, alternating personalities have been so caused. This is the case of Thomas Hanna,[29] 'a young clergymen of good education and sound health',[30] who had a bad fall, came to with no memory, and then for some years followed the alternating pattern of Mary Reynolds. But there is one important difference between them. Hanna seems to have had no emotional stress of any kind or any history of hysteria that might foreshadow a split. It seems entirely due to his fall; and his two personalities, most unusually, were not different in character. They simply alternated with mutual amnesia. In fact it might be better not to call this a case of dissociated personality at all, only of dissociated memory systems. Generally the difference in character is striking. One personality in a set may be highly moral and the other irresponsible, like EW and EB, B₁ and Sally, A and B of BCA. They may claim (and behave as) different ages or sexes. One may be respectable and one criminal, one sane and the other mad: 'Emile X . . . in one personality was a respectable lawyer, but in the other was destructive and a gambler, swindler, and thief; . . . Sörgel . . . in one personality was quiet, pious and industrious. In the other personality he was insane, often violent, and assaultive, and one time chopped an old wood-cutter to death and drank his blood.'³¹ Or one may simply be conventional and timid while the other is bolder, with higher spirits and more scope: MR₁ and MR₂. And in such cases (so far as I know) the split has no independent physical cause, though it may come after an unusually long sleep. Where a shock seems to lead to it, it is emotional, not physical: something which the new self either retreats from in an exaggerated way, or which it can cope with where the old self could not.³²

In BCA the B complex seems to have been a distillation of C's rebellious feelings against a hard life nursing a sick husband. C seems to have tried to suppress these feelings, and their only expression was in daydreams; the split allowed this side to take over BCA's behaviour entirely, when B was 'out'. BCA is rare in that there was so much of B — enough to make a distinct personality from A, first in feeling and action, later in memory and consciousness as well. (B became to A as EB was to EW.) But we might expect lesser and more common dissociations, when nothing independent seems to cause them, to follow a like pattern: that is, to grow out of moral or temperamental conflict in a person. And notoriously they seem to: the best collection of examples is probably (still) Freud's *Psychopathology of Everyday Life*.³³

Freud of course takes the dissociated thought to be unconscious. His is the best-known view of such behaviour and also (perhaps) the most widely accepted. It is the alternative to the one I have considered so far — a Bx or Dx that works consciously — and I want now to consider it.

It is not the only theory that his premises will allow, not to mention his data. Take for example the standard argument for the existence of a (repressed) unconscious mind, as given in *The Ego and the Id*: 'The term "conscious" is, to start with, a purely descriptive one, resting on a perception of the most direct and certain character'. (There are logical problems here: the idea of directly perceiving that a thought is conscious seems confused. But let us take the main argument first.)

Experience shows, next, that a mental element (for instance, an idea) is not as a rule permanently conscious. . . . An idea that is conscious now is no longer so a moment later, although it can become so again under certain conditions that are easily brought about. . . . We can say it was *latent*, and by this we mean *capable of becoming conscious at any time*. Or, if we say that it was *unconscious*, we are giving an equally correct description.

. . . But we have arrived at the term or concept of 'unconscious' along another path. . . . We have found, that is, we have been obliged to assume, that very powerful mental processes or ideas exist . . . which can produce in the mind all the effects that ordinary ideas do (including effects that can in turn become conscious as ideas) without themselves becoming conscious. It is unnecessary here to repeat in detail what has been explained so often before. We need only say that this is the point at which psychoanalytic theory steps in — with the assertion that such ideas cannot become conscious because a certain force is opposed to them, that otherwise they would be conscious. . . . The fact that in the technique of psychoanalysis a means has been found by which the opposing force can be removed and the ideas in question made conscious renders this theory irrefutable.[34]

Irrefutable perhaps, but not proven. All that Freud's argument entails is that ideas of which the *dominant* self was not conscious are at last made available to it. We have no reason to assume *a priori* that a single integrated Ego must know all the conscious thoughts any human being has — in fact, multiple personality shows us that sometimes this is clearly not so. It follows that some if not all the 'unconscious' thoughts released in psychoanalysis may have been not unconscious, but conscious and dissociated. (Freud's own thoughts may have turned this way at the end. His last essay — unfinished — is called 'The Splitting of the Ego'.[35])

Let me go back now to Freud's statement that conciousness is a thing that we perceive. His theory demands that there should be both conscious and unconscious thought. Consciousness will therefore have to be a property which is not necessary to thought but can pertain to it, as blueness can pertain to some eyes. We can perceive that a person's eyes are blue and in a like way, Freud seems to say, we can perceive that certain thoughts are conscious.

But even if we were to grant that consciousness is a nonessential property of thought, it is not one that we could perceive. Since we cannot directly perceive other people's thoughts, the 'perception' that a given thought is conscious can only be introspection — which is usually (if not always) retrospection. In short, we usually if not always come to know our thoughts' properties through memory. I shall come back to this point; but suppose first that we can also introspect present thoughts (in a 'specious present'). I am not fond of the word 'perceive' here, but I can think of a sense in which I might claim to 'perceive' that a thought is vague, or an after-image, or about music, or in French. The one thing that I cannot possibly 'perceive' is that it is conscious. For the thoughts that I 'perceive' will be conscious if and only if *I* am conscious *of* them; and I must *a priori* be conscious of them if I can 'perceive' them at all.

It does not matter what properties I 'perceive' them to have. My thoughts, taken all together, might have no single property in common: if I perceive *that*, these thoughts must all be conscious. Or again: it is hard to see how one would ever notice a property that was always there, whenever one noticed a thought at all. But suppose for the sake of argument that all conscious thought seemed to share one quality: it might perhaps vary in degree, and be noticeable because of that. If I 'perceived' this quality, it could not be consciousness, but only something that always goes with it. For it would be part of the content of my 'perception'; but I say that a thought is conscious for a reason that is independent of content. The claim that I can directly perceive that a thought is conscious amounts in fact to much the same thing as that I can directly perceive my own mind, or mental substance, or myself as a thinking thing; and my objection to it amounts to much the same as Hume's objection to the others.[36]

As for retrospection: the only reason why I can say that a past thought was conscious is (by retrospection) that I can remember it. That of course is not a necessary condition, since I have had, I suppose, any number of conscious thoughts which I cannot now remember. I know about those through public evidence, if at all: the kind anyone else must use who wants to learn about my thoughts. We might go on however to ask if memory is a sufficient condition either. Usually we take this for granted; but both hypnosis and psychoanalysis are said sometimes to release mental records of things past, *when there is in fact no evidence at all that these records were consciously made.* We may also be able to recall things that we unconsciously perceived, with no such artificial aids, especially if we have a good visual memory. *'Cast your mind back, Madame'* says Hercule

Poirot. '*At the time you were not conscious of anything unusual, perhaps. But call to your mind the image of the library, when you first walked in: can you tell me now if there is in it anything odd, or not as it should be?*'

We may in fact speak of recollection in three different ways. (1) We could take it as an axiom that any mental record which can later become conscious must be of a thing consciously recorded, even if only in a flash. (2) We may say that we will not call it a memory, when someone becomes conscious of a record unconsciously made. (We might in the same way refuse to call an innate idea a memory.) If we do this, we shall need a new word for the records that were unconsciously made; and often we will have no idea whether it or 'memory' is right in a given case. (3) We may decide to use 'memory' for any recollection of the past, however it happens. It will then mean less to say that we remember a thing than we now usually suppose.

(Whichever line we take, we could also on occasion decide instead that no record was made: if it is somebody else he may be mistaken or lying, if ourself we may be mistaken. This need not affect the main issue, since it is not credible that all claims to remember can be mistakes or lies; but the chance of it makes it unlikely that generalizations about memory are based on fact alone. This is most notably so if the 'memory' in question is supposed to be of something like a childhood fantasy, which was repressed.)

I see no reason why we should make the assumptions demanded by (1). (2) and (3) however leave the issue as open as before.

There is one more point that I should make here. I have said that 'perceiving that a thought is conscious' does not make sense, *even if we suppose that consciousness is a nonessential property of thought*. But if 'thought' were taken to entail 'mental rather than physical' (as traditionally it often has been) of course I could not say this. Since I see no reason why there should exist an immaterial substance, 'mind', I can only distinguish the mental from the physical by distinguishing *experience* from any brain process or behaviour which it accompanies. Unconscious thought would then be certain brain processes (and perhaps behaviour) which have no concomitant experience, distinguished from other such bodily processes as Freud suggests in the passage that I quoted: by their relation to thought which is conscious. Unconscious thought, if we so define it, would count neither as 'mental' nor as 'thought' by the traditional standard. But in fact I would never define 'thought' in that way. It is a more elastic term than that, and less theory-laden.

Now that I have said that I think unconscious thoughts are bodily processes, I want to go back to the thesis that Bx and Dx are unconscious. The argument against it would be that both Example 4 and D have a lot in common with more extreme dissociations: Eve, Miss Beauchamp and so on; and there a co-conscious agent seems to pull the strings. But a different functional model suggests a different view. (That is the trouble with models.) There are computers. Computers can record and react, selectively and towards an end. They can adjust how they will later react, and in general rearrange their program, by negative feedback from a changing situation. A computer can for example *learn* to play draughts or chess by trial and error, starting (as we do) with only the basic rules, the aim to win (by not repeating mistakes) and a series of opponents to practise on.[37] Unless we beg the question and insist that if anything can do that, it must be conscious, this would seem to show that Bx (and more importantly, Dx) could just as well work unconsciously.

What we can *know* about B in Example 4 is this: he is deceived at least in the sense of 'The clear air deceived me . . .', since he is not aware of the truth. He thinks that what makes him open the window is that the room is stuffy and hot. And what blocks any awareness of the hypnotist's suggestion from him (that is, from BW) must be some part of himself. We can also say about D that he may not be the only type we would accuse of self-deception, but he is a common one; and he could in theory work like B. In each case the deceiving factor would then be a dissociated 'splinter' or complex.

We have both an unconscious and a conscious model for our splinter. The next step obviously is to see which model fits; then we will know how far the deceiving factor is literally a deceiver. Unfortunately the next step is impossible. I have sorted out the arguments for each side into a dialogue that will (I hope) show why. My Philonous and Hylas are not the same as Berkeley's, but the names fit just as well.

PHILONOUS: Of course Bx and Dx work consciously. Look at Sally Beauchamp and Eve Black.

HYLAS: We don't know they are like Sally Beauchamp and Eve Black in this way, simply because they are like them in others. By a different analogy, they might work like a programmed computer.

PHILONOUS: But Bx is continuous with BH — must be, since Bx does what BH is told to do. Surely BH is conscious.

HYLAS: If you mean that BH *must* be conscious in order to hear the instruction — no, why be dogmatic? Even if a man later remembers something that he was told, he may have taken it in unconsciously. On the other hand, there is no reason to think that BH is *not* conscious. He is in hypnosis; but this can allow behaviour whose consciousness no one would normally doubt.

But what if he is? It doesn't mean Bx must be. B could have heard the instruction consciously, but followed it automatically. We do something of the sort when we walk along a path that we know well, while thinking about something quite different.

PHILONOUS: It's not clear, in a case like that, that our conscious thoughts *are* all on something different. We may simply not remember the ones that guide our feet. The only time we get an inside story on 'automatic' behaviour is when it turns up in a case of multiple personality — and then we find a co-conscious agent.

HYLAS: A co-conscious *personality*, which Bx and Dx are not. Had it occurred to you that these might be the only times we get an inside story, simply because only a full personality has an 'inside'? What does it even mean to say that a *splinter* like Bx is conscious?

PHILONOUS: I mean that Bx is a stream of conscious thought, cut off from the main one.

HYLAS: I understand 'conscious person' and in rare cases

'personality'; *derivatively* from them I understand 'conscious thought'. The idea of a separate splinter or stream that is conscious in its own right means nothing to me, especially when all that it seems to do is pour and swallow drinks, or register nine hand-in-pockets and open a window.

PHILONOUS: Here is something more familiar. Suppose that I have to be up by nine. I am asleep and a clock strikes nine, and I automatically leap up. This is reacting like Bx to a remembered plan ('Be up by nine') and a counted signal. You say that the signal may be taken in unconsciously: well, if I can't remember taking it in I've no argument against you. I'm like BW who can't remember. But sometimes I do remember: I keep a clear impression of hearing the clock. And it may be *all* that I remember — which shows I was conscious only of that. Isn't this a splinter of the kind I mean?

HYLAS: I've already said that I don't think memory guarantees past consciousness. But suppose that you were conscious: how do you know that you were conscious only of the clock? You might *either* have registered the clock mechanically, while fast asleep, *or* been conscious of a lot more which you forgot.

PHILONOUS: Still if that is my clear impression, the onus is surely on you —

HYLAS: It's quite easy to find clear impressions that support my view instead. I know a Professor who fell asleep at a philosophy seminar and woke to hear somebody say 'Yes, what *would* Professor X say to that?' He produced an answer (he says) out of his unconscious, which seemed to get by. *His* impression was that he had taken the question in unconsciously, well enough to give an answer of sorts: a more complicated reaction than jumping out of bed on the stroke of nine.

But my objection goes further. Consciousness (*pace* Freud) can't be a quality that one observes in a thought. So whatever your 'clear impression' is, it can't be exactly of *that*.

PHILONOUS: If so, the same thing goes for unconsciousness. Your Professor X couldn't argue from *his* impression —

HYLAS: If anything I have said suggests that he would, I apologize to him. I only brought him in to show that not even impressions agree about cases like these.

My final objection is that you say *you* were conscious only of the clock. You can put it this way only if *you* remember this, that is relate it to other conscious thoughts of *yours* later on — even if you didn't at the time. BW on the other hand does not remember Bx; and this makes Bx essentially different.

PHILONOUS: Why? Take any ordinary time when one consciously hears a clock strike nine (say) and leaps out of bed. You'll at least admit that happens?

HYLAS: I'll even admit that it often *seems* to happen when one is half asleep and aware only of the clock. So what?

PHILONOUS: Someone who does that will only know that he consciously heard the clock if he remembers it. (You say that this may not be enough to establish consciousness, but at least it's what people usually go by.) But surely whenever someone remembers a thing, it's also possible in theory that he might *not* have remembered it, while everything else about it stays the same. Then nobody would know that the thought was a conscious one; but it would be.

HYLAS: Not if 'conscious' is the kind of predicate I think. You seem to be saying that we can't call a person or a personality conscious — or a lesser complex of thoughts — unless we can call its constituent thoughts each conscious in its own right. You might as well say that a hill can't be half a mile high or conical unless you can say the same for each of its parts.

Relation I think is of the essence. It's not just that I can't say *I* was conscious at such a time unless I remember it — which is to relate my thought then to my thought now. If *you* leap out of bed when a clock strikes, I can't start to decide what I think of *your* state until I can relate your leap to other signs of consciousness. If you fall right back again snoring and give no further sign that you heard it, I'll probably decide that you weren't conscious after all when you leaped up, of the clock or anything else. It was just a reflex.

PHILONOUS: You might be wrong, though. I might be pretending, for a start. . . . But even if relation between thoughts is of the essence, it can't *be* the essence — at least not if memory is your paradigm for such relations. As you said just now, we may 'remember' things taken in unconsciously. 'Why be dogmatic?' you said.

And now *I* shall attack *you*.

By your own argument a *complex* of thoughts might be conscious, even if it were less than a full personality. And by your own argument, even what seems to be an isolated splinter could in fact connect to thoughts that are forgotten. For Bx we even have a connection: BH. As for Dx: when a dissociation obviously has a function, and when it involves a long series of acts or goes on for a long time, I think that we may assume a complex, and quite a full one.

I like my model better than yours because (other things being equal) I think that one human is probably more like another, even an abnormal one, than like a machine. And other things *are* equal. You could not prove *your* theory without a principle stating the necessary unity (or 'transparency') of consciousness; and the multiple personality cases show that this is illegitimate. You are no better off than I am.

The conclusion is: *in principle inconclusive*. This is because of how we identify Bx and Dx.

Suppose that a man has had a fall. Someone asks 'Is he conscious?' and I look. Are his eyes open? Does he seem to hear what we say? Does he answer coherently? And so on. His consciousness at a past time may in the same way be decided from reports of what he did, or I may ask him if he remembers it. (As Philonous says, that is at least a thing we usually go by.) And now suppose that I want to know about some particular thought, or proposition: is he conscious that p? I look to see if he acts as though p in some way or other, including talk. The evidence, as we have seen, may sometimes be inconclusive or puzzling; it may even seem paradoxical. But at least I know where to look. The same is true if I want to know whether he knew or believed that p at some past time: I go by reports (or my memory) of his past behaviour and speech, and also by what he now says and remembers.

None of this is any use when I must decide about a dissociated Bx of Dx. For simplicity I shall use 'Ax' for the splinter from now on, and 'A' for the person. Ax has no behaviour of its own, that we know independently: we have simply decided to describe some of A's behaviour in terms of it. This is one thing that makes it quite unlike a dissociated personality. Ax's memory is out of reach: we define it as Ax's precisely because A — the main A — seems unaware of it. If he later recalls it and says that he was aware of it at the time, we must redefine it not as Ax's memory but as A's. If he later recalls it but says that he was not aware of it at the time, or that he does not know if he was or not, we are no wiser than before about whether Ax was at that time conscious. So we can only favour Hylas over Philonous or *vice versa* on principle, or analogy, or intuition. This is useless: what we wanted to know in the first place was which analogy fits, which intuition is sound, which principle (if any) to adopt.

When it comes to understanding self-deception this has an odd result. We have examples of full consciousness and (I think) full unconsciousness — in Eve Black and a chess-playing computer — each of which 'acts' enough like A's Ax side to be like it at this point. Consciousness may also be a matter of degree, so that there are half-conscious states. This would fit the idea that it depends somehow on the complexity of interrelated thoughts. Nor does there seem to be any reason why all Axs should be the same, especially if complexity is important. And we have at least this much evidence that it is: the dissociated systems that we *know* to be conscious are the most complex ones of all, the dissociated personalities. I would agree with Hylas that below the level where Ax may be called a *complex*, 'conscious' has a clear use only derivatively.

So we have reason to say of any Ax that it falls somewhere in this range; but we cannot say where. It follows that *we can never know, for a self-deception of this kind, whether it is literally a deception or not.*

There is one last point. We have seen that if A does literally deceive himself, this will be because deceiver and victim are separate aspects of A. I suggested 'A bites himself' as an analogy. It should now be clear that the analogy is a bad one. If I say 'A bites B', A-the-Biter is the same when B is A as when he is not. And if I say 'A bites A' the bitten part will be something (an arm or whatever) that A could also bite in somebody else. But 'A deceives A' seems to work only if we define A-the-Deceiver as a dissociated Ax, which we would not do if we said that A deceived anybody else; the same kind of thing is true strictly (if less conspicuously) of A-the-Deceived. 'A deceives himself' turns out in fact to be more like 'A bites himself in the teeth' with all the problems that this raises.

In short, Ax *ex hypothesi* is not a distinct 'self', as a dissociated personality would be; but neither can we say that Ax is *A himself*, the A who would deceive in the usual way. This seems to show that 'self-deception' can never be reflexive enough to be taken literally. Philonous' line (which makes 'deception' literal) will not save it any better than Hylas' (which does not)— even if we knew which line to take.

5 BAD FAITH AND SOME ALTERNATIVES

THE best-known philosophical theory of self-deception is almost certainly that of Jean-Paul Sartre. He works it out most fully in *L'Etre et le néant* (*Being and Nothingness*),[38] but the theme runs through most of his work, including novels, like *La nausée*, and plays, like *Huis clos*. His name for what he discusses is '*Mauvaise foi*': literally, 'bad faith'. This is something less than 'self-deception'; for I take 'faith' to mean a commitment to feel and to act, rather than a belief in the epistemological sense. Some of Sartre's thesis seems coloured by this difference. On the other hand he defines '*mauvaise foi*' as 'lying to oneself'[39] and on the whole discusses it in these terms. Some translators of Sartre use 'self-deception' for '*mauvaise foi*' (Philip Mairet for example in *Existentialism and Humanism*[40]) and I think that this is perfectly fair.

Sartre's theory of self-deception is grounded in his general theory of Being: the system that he develops in *Being and Nothingness*. I shall not go into this at length. Certain key arguments may (I think) be understood and discussed on their own, and this is what I shall do. I shall also come back at several points to the famous examples in his chapter 'Patterns of Bad Faith'.

Let us start with the question that I have already quoted: '. . . *How then can the lie subsist, if the duality that conditions it is suppressed?*' Sartre believes that the self-deceiver is not divided. He argues in *Being and Nothingness* that dissociation (of the kind I refer to in Chapter 4) is impossible. His argument is aimed specifically against Freud; but it would rule out a 'Philonous' thesis too, if it worked. It rests on two main premisses:

I. Any mental element that could deceive the conscious mind must itself be conscious.

II. Consciousness is totally translucent, so that one part can never hide its workings from another.

The argument for Premiss I is in *Being and Nothingness*, Chapter 2. Freud, Sartre says, reports resistance by the patient, as the doctor draws near a true interpretation of his neurosis. What is it that resists? It is not the Ego ('envisioned as a psychic totality of the facts of consciousness'). It cannot recognize the true interpretation for what it is: this is why the patient needs an analyst. Moreover the patient goes to the analyst by choice, that is, by the Ego's choice. If the Ego were to resist what it itself has chosen, it would be in bad faith; but this conclusion is what the psychoanalytic theory is framed to avoid. Nor is it the repressed complex: 'The complex as such is rather the collaborator of the psychoanalyst since it aims at expressing itself in clear consciousness, since it plays tricks on the censor and seeks to elude it'. Clearly it is the censore. But

If we reject the language and materialist mythology of psychoanalysis, we perceive that the censor in order to apply its activity with discernment must know what it is repressing . . .. It must also appreciate the condemned drives as *to be repressed* . . .. To know is to know that one knows, said Alain. Let us say rather: All knowing is consciousness of knowing. Thus the resistance of the patient implies on the level of the censor an awareness of the thing repressed as such, a comprehension of the end toward which it compares the *truth* of the repressed complex to the psychoanalytic hypothesis which aims at it. These various operations in their turn imply that the censor is conscious (of) itself . . .. Its consciousness must be of the drive to be repressed, but precisely *in order not to be conscious of it*. What does this mean if not that the censor is in bad faith?

Psychoanalysis has not gained anything . . . in order to overcome bad faith, it has established between the unconscious and the consciousness an autonomous consciousness in bad faith.[41]

I would make the following comments. (1) The complex need not always aim at 'expressing itself in clear consciousness' when it plays tricks: it may aim at playing tricks. Robin Hood no doubt did not outlaw himself; but after a few years learning the tricks of the greenwood, would he necessarily want to give them up? A 'Freudian slip' for example, if it is well-timed, may sometimes spoil what one is consciously trying to do far more effectively than any unwillingness which one openly knows and accepts. The only thing that we *must* expect a complex to aim at, if it includes a rebellion against doing X, is spoiling X; and a neurosis may put it in a state of power here, *vis-à-vis* the Ego —

or at least into a state of equilibrium. Why indeed should we try to make it conscious in analysis, if not to disarm it? (2) Suppose that the censor is conscious, as Sartre suggests. Why must it be conscious of the condemned drive 'as to be repressed . . . in order not to be conscious of it?' It is less tortuous to suppose that the censor wants the *Ego* not to be conscious of it. In short the censor, if conscious, would be not in bad faith, but a liar. This could fit (1). (3) *'All knowing is consciousness of knowing'*: 'consciousness' must be dispositional here, or this rules out even the (surely) unproblematic knowledge that Freud calls 'preconscious' or 'latent' (see above, page 43). I think it must mean what I myself would mean if I said 'All knowledge is free knowledge'. If so, Sartre is claiming that the censor must become conscious, at every (or nearly every) appropriate time, of the drive to be repressed, etc. He also assumes that such times of consciousness *must* occur whenever the censor is suppressing this forbidden material.

But we can turn Hylas' computer analogy against Sartre here. The censor's work seems to be, in effect, screening, and also re-adapting its methods and aims to new data that come in. (I see no reason at all why it should need anything like the philosophical concept of truth that Sartre attributes to it.) We could argue that many 'intelligent' machines were conscious, using terms like 'knowledge', 'discernment', 'awareness', 'comprehension' with no worse *functional* grounds than Sartre's about the censor; and functional grounds are all that anyone can have, unless the censor turns out to be an Eve Black 'picking out' memories, and telling us about it later. In fact there exists at least one computer program simulating a Freudian-type neurosis,[42] not with complete success, but successfully enough (I think) to undermine Sartre here. There is still the programmer to consider; but what in the censor's work could not be 'programmed' by the individual's genes and life history, though no conscious planner was at work? Nothing obvious enough (surely) to rule out this alternative; for our purely physiological development as we grow up demands, on the face of it, at least as complicated a program, and one which we seem not to design.

I doubt if Sartre could accept the other way out: the idea that some machines are conscious too. This would make them

'Beings-for-Themselves' with the freedom and responsibility that he thinks this entails; and this does not mix very well with their being built and programmed by human beings. But if he will not accept *that* — in the face of what we know about computers — he cannot have (I) as an axiom.

Premiss II, the translucency principle, seems to be essential to Sartre's thesis. The argument that follows his question 'How can the lie subsist . . .?' is typical:

> To this difficulty [that I must know the truth very accurately in order to conceal it more carefully] is added another which is derived from the total translucency of consciousness. That which affects itself with bad faith must be conscious (of) its bad faith, since the being of consciousness is the consciousness of being. It appears then that I must be in good faith, at least to the extent that I am conscious of my bad faith. But then the whole psychic system is annihilated. We must agree in fact that if I deliberately and cynically lie to myself, I fail completely in the undertaking; the lie falls back and collapses beneath my look . . .. The very consciousness of lying to myself . . . pitilessly constitutes itself well within my project as its very condition.[43]

Insofar as this argues that the whole individual cannot (univocally) be said to deceive himself, I agree: my second chapter should make that clear. But the reason is not that an individual's consciousness must be an integrated whole, because consciousness is translucent. There is no need for any analysis of concepts here, of the kind that seems to give Sartre his thesis. Eve Black/Eve White and their kind disprove the translucency principle by existing, so that if our concept of consciousness entails translucency, it is wrong.

Given the one-way mental access that we find in pairs like these, we can save the translucency principle only by making it empty. We could insist that since Eve White had no access to the thoughts of Eve Black, they must by definition be separate consciousnesses. Eve Black's access to Eve White's thoughts must then be declared (by definition) not immediate, however it may seem to Eve Black: some unexplained medium must communicate them. This is uselessly mysterious and I know of no evidence to support it, but it cannot (of course) be proved false. But then the translucency principle will never tell us when somebody is in bad faith. Even if premiss I were true, he could always in theory be two consciousnesses, one deceiving the other.

I suspect however that Sartre would try to take another way

out. He seems to hold that a Being-for-Itself is responsible for anything that happens to its mind, if this has some emotional function. Even fainting in a crisis is to lose consciousness by choice, because it allows a kind of 'magical' escape.[44] He would therefore say that Eve's split has to be her conscious choice, and is a kind of of bad faith. Since bad faith is also by his account a paradox, this is probably the least reasonable explanation we can get. A Sartre-saving alternative would be to say that Eve's split is a deliberate fake, and so are all cases like her: again a lot to swallow. It seems more sensible to give up premiss II.

There is also of course all the evidence we have for repression in everyday life. I know in my own case of many word-slips, lapses of memory and the like which it is very hard to explain in other terms; so do most people, I suspect. In terms of repression they are only too easy to explain: more often than not (when I notice them) they seem very clearly to reveal thoughts or wishes that I know I have been trying to suppress. When I do not see this, other people often do, and tell me. I am as sure as I can be that I — main conscious I — neither plan nor foresee these slips; indeed by any rule but the question-begging one that says we always do what we really want, they are often the last thing I want. For example: a friend once asked me to lend him quite a lot of money, by our standards. I could do it, I did not grudge him the money, had been helped by him in the past, in general wanted him to have it. I also did not want to be someone to whom he owed that much. I did not know when he would be able to pay it back and while he could not, his pride might suffer and so (I was afraid) might our relationship. All the rest outweighed this misgiving however, and I felt rather ashamed of worrying about it, so I set out to ignore it: lend the money and (of course) never show that I was worried. As I was writing the cheque the telephone rang, I answered it, came back and sent the cheque off unsigned — a thing I have never done with a cheque before or after. If all of us who seem to remember self-sabotage of this kind really chose it in bad faith, why does it seem so different? Do we now mask it with more bad faith? That is Sartre's idea, but by his own argument, the mask is never impenetrable. The opposite of bad faith is sincerity. Practising it as hard as I can, I insist from my own experience that it can be impenetrable; that consciousness is not translucent, or else there are unconscious mental processes that play tricks and repress; in short that in cases like these we really do not know what we are doing — except perhaps under some description that hides its real aim.

Of course particular cases are hard to prove. When there is any doubt, we tend to disown unworthiness as far as we can, even if it is no farther than our own unconscious. This may make us uneasy in practice almost any time that somebody says 'I didn't mean it, it was unconscious', especially if this means that we can no longer blame him for something that we resent. But even if we doubt him, one form that the doubt often takes is about memory: is he repressing now the fact that he was not repressing before? (We can ask the same thing about ourselves.)

I shall treat repression then as not only possible, but a fact — so long as we leave the Hylas/Philonous question open. I think it is a notable flaw in Sartre's theory that he will not allow for it. But he is still right, I think, to hold that neither 'bad faith' nor 'lying to oneself' nor (I would add) 'self-deception' means that fact. Repression is not a paradoxical idea, whatever Sartre may think; 'lying to oneself' (etc.) suggest one that is.

I think it is a strength in Sartre that he takes this seriously. We use these paradoxical terms as though we felt that they alone do justice to what we see. But in spite of (I think partly because of) an elaborate metaphysic of consciousness, and many shrewd half-hints when he describes behaviour, he never takes the next step: to show logically how this apparent contradiction in terms comes true. Paradox is often epigrammatic and he has a weakness for epigram, as well as for that lofty 'philosophic' style that can so dangerously mask the vague or empty concept, the banal or inconclusive conclusion. I agree with Fingarette when he complains:

Can one and the same 'unified' consciousness both believe and not believe? On this issue, Sartre's concluding definitive words are that the 'structure' of *mauvaise foi* is 'of the metastable type' (p. 68); it consists in an 'inner disintegration in the heart of being' (p. 70). In short we are given esoteric labels rather than a resolution of the dilemma.[45]

Sartre states and restates the *problem* in many forms: I have quoted one already, here and in Chapter 1. Another way argues that if we look for the first moment of bad faith, we seem to find an infinite regress: 'At the very moment when I was disposed to put myself in bad faith, I was of necessity in bad faith with respect to this same disposition. For me to have represented it to myself as bad faith would have been cynicism; to believe it sincerely innocent would have been in good faith.'[46] This suggests that we must be born in bad faith, and in general there is a look of original sin about the idea as Sartre describes it (one obscure concept reflecting another). But he says that we put ourselves into bad faith, we are not born in it; it remains for him therefore to explain how.

Insofar as he explains, Sartre tries to have it all ways. He says that we are in bad faith when we decide to put ourselves in bad faith; but this 'decision' is not a 'reflective, voluntary decision' but a 'spontaneous determination of our being'. He also compares it to falling asleep; but what he says exactly is 'One *puts oneself* in bad faith as one goes to sleep and one is in bad faith as one dreams.'[47] This is misleading: we do not *put* ourselves to sleep, unless this means taking a drug or using self-hypnosis. We do hold people responsible sometimes for going to sleep; but the responsibility is either for taking steps so that sleep will come, or for failing to stay awake — as a nurse might fall asleep on night duty. Neither of these seems strong enough for Sartre's position, although I think he is right to suggest that both in fact have parallels in self-deception. They certainly have in wishful thinking. In Sartre's defence we might say that real sleep and dreams ought to be different, by his account, from what we usually think: if fainting can be a choice, why not sleep? But (oddly perhaps) he does not press this; and if he did, this would make sleep more mysterious by assimilating it to bad faith, rather than clarifying bad faith by comparing it to sleep. As for 'spontaneous determination of our being', 'spontaneous' is as vague as Demos' 'yielding to impulse', although (like that phrase) it may slightly favour the view that lying to oneself is an act. We talk of giving a spontaneous cry, but not of spontaneously sneezing. 'Determination' is as vague, but perhaps biassed the other way, towards 'determinism'. The whole passage is ambiguous from beginning to end (and this is not the fault of the translation).

One thing however is clear in Sartre's thesis: the man in bad faith tries to avoid a truth, and he does this by redescription — or perhaps sometimes a parallel way of thinking that uses no

words, but may still be called 'representation'. The aim is to see
things differently rather than not to see. And this seems right to
me on the whole. Mr D for instance does not deny the drink in
his hand when it is pointed out to him, but tries to interpret it in
a way that makes him still 'really' a light, evening drinker. He
feels that his wife's bare statement — and the barer one that she
implies — do not put his case fairly. Sartre also says that what
we typically redescribe in bad faith is ourselves: in one of
several possible ways we claim to be what we are not. Trivially
this must be so: if I do not want to face the fact that p, I must
change all descriptions of myself which imply that I *know* that
p. More than this is less evident. The self-deceiving mother for
example (let us call her Mrs M) will probably redescribe her son
as D redescribes himself. Her son is a good boy 'really'. This or
that misdeed that he was caught doing was due to accident or
bad luck or evil influence or at worst foolishness. It is unfair to
make the obvious inferences about him . . .. Sartre calls this
attitude (applied to oneself) one of 'perpetual disintegration
. . . so that we may slide at any time from naturalistic present to
transcendence and *vice versa*'.[48]

Roughly, a conscious being transcends what it (naturalisti-
cally) is at a given time, in that it is not bound by its present state
as a mere thing would be. It is free to create its own nature, and
this, so long as it lives, is never final. To keep one's present state
(say that of a man who drinks too much) is a possible choice, but
we are no more forced to make it than any other. Sartre seems to
hold that this is true of all conscious beings, and that to be
conscious entails being conscious of that fact. But we need not
follow him so far, to find this passage interesting. He goes on:

We can see the use bad faith can make of those judgments which all aim at
establishing that I am not what I am. If I were only what I *am*, I could, for
example, seriously consider an adverse criticism which someone makes of me,
question myself scrupulously, and perhaps be compelled to recognize the
truth in it. But thanks to transcendence, I am not subject to all that I am. I do
not even have to discuss the justice of the reproach . . .. I am on a plane where
no reproach can touch me, since what I really am is my transcendence. I flee
from myself, I escape myself, I leave my tattered garment in the hands of the
fault-finder. But the ambiguity necessary for bad faith comes from the fact
that I affirm here that I *am* my transcendence in the mode of being a thing.[49]

If Sartre is right, we might say of Mr D that he knows he is *not* a
man who drinks too much as he is (say) a man of blood group B.

He therefore illegitimately claims that he *is*, in the blood-group sense, a man who does *not* drink too much. And so just as there is nothing that he can do to change his blood group, there is nothing that he need do to change his drinking.

If this is supposed to be D's explicit thought, it seems too subtle for the ordinary drinking man. But it does (I think) follow a familiar pattern of self-deception in an intellectualized way. Without putting it in terms of different modes of being, D may well vaguely feel that he is not really a man who drinks too much because — perhaps not long ago — he *was* not. This gives him a total picture of himself in which drinking too much is not a necessary part; so it must be accidental, a thing that can change at any time. Again D is not likely to put it as Sartre does, in terms of consciousnesses *versus* things: apart from the far-fetched terminology, it would follow that *no* drunk was ever 'really' so. Sartre does think this; but I suspect that the average D is likelier to draw comparisons. 'Now Simpkin is a real drunk. Hopeless. But look at Smith: he drank more last year than I do now. Just a phase. Got him through a bad patch. *He's* not a real alcoholic.' 'Real' alcoholics however are like things in the relevant way: not free to change.

Sartre's 'slide from facticity to transcendence and back' explains nothing here, if D is supposed to know that this is what he does and yet (somehow) come to believe his own lie. Buried knowledge would explain it, but not if 'All knowing is con- sciousness of knowing', so that buried knowledge does not exist. But if D thinks as I now suggest, perhaps he need not believe what he says ('Really I only drink in the evenings, you know that') in its usual sense; and it is this sense that we would normally mean if we said that he must know it is false. Suppose that instead of taking words like 'really' to apply to what he is just now, he is thinking of a *whole* D, including a temperate past and a temperate future. (The temperate future is no doubt wishful thinking; I shall come back to that.) He does not tell his wife that he means this and may not word it clearly to himself; and (like B of BCA) he could know that there is something eccentric about his claim. But we need not therefore suppose that he does not believe it, and know that he believes it. His believing his words in some sense, but not the usual one, may give him that air of defensive sincerity often seen in self- deceivers.

Why then does he put it this way, which is bound to mislead? There are several likely reasons that do not lead to paradox. It takes skill to say such things clearly when no ready-made formula exists; many people — most people maybe — do not have this. And even if D has the skill, it usually takes time to think the words out; he is in a hurry to answer his wife. It also takes effort, and it is natural enough to avoid effort, other things being equal; it is also natural to avoid subjects that one dislikes, and D can hardly like this one. Even if in fact he felt secure — in some real way *not* a man who drinks too much — it is annoying to have to justify oneself; and he almost certainly does not feel secure. (Feeling is not knowing, however: we are still this side of paradox.) In particular he will be annoyed with his wife, who interprets what she sees not in his way but at face value; and so he is not likely to take trouble for her sake, and likely to feel that it serves her right if she does not understand. If she were not being suspicious and ungenerous she would.

Like BCA's then, D's self-deception seems not a matter of knowledge denied, but of judgments that he will not accept. On the other hand, *his* way of meaning his words may be false too, and in a way that he recognizes. If so the problem has only moved a step back; but is it so?

D's 'slide from facticity to transcendence and back' might occur to him in some such form as: 'People like Smith and me are always free to stop, and therefore in time we're bound to'. This shows up rather too crudely the ambiguity on which (Sartre says) the self-deceiver trades, but it expands into something more natural: (1) 'People like Smith and me stop drinking when we really want to' plus (2) 'In time one is bound really to want to'.

Neither (1) nor (2) is well grounded. (1) raises if-can problems: we cannot take *really wanting* as a sure sign of success unless we (trivially) say 'He really wanted to' only after somebody succeeds. In this example I make D restrict (1) to what we might call the Smith type, which may give it a look of greater plausibility at first sight; but if Smith's only relevant feature is having succeeded, this counts for nothing. D himself has not yet succeeded, so he cannot claim to be a Smith type; but the truth of (1) depends on this. (Of course he may sometimes have other grounds for saying that he is a Smith type. But if they are good ones, we would not call this self-deception.) Sartre would say that (1) is true because, in the relevant way, we are all Smith types; but if D rules out Simpkin, D cannot say this. Sartre has theories about freewill to which I shall come back later. I have framed (1) however to be ambiguous on this point, as I think common usage and common thinking are.

I framed (2) loosely because again this seemed natural: 'one' can mean 'I' or 'my type' or 'anyone' or (very likely) waver from one sense to another. But in any case D's grounds for (2) will probably be just the usual idea that it is bad to go on drinking as much as D. This will not support the sense of 'really want' that guarantees success in stopping.

If D must know that his beliefs can be so faulted, he is in trouble. But why must he? Criticism of this kind takes thought, so here too it is important that many people dislike such thought and may need no further motive to avoid it. If it is also about an unpleasant subject, we all have a motive. If D therefore does not know what is wrong with (1) and (2), he is probably guilty of laziness, and the laziness allows him wishful thinking; he is also to blame for speaking (inconsiderately) in a way that misleads, for judging his wife unfairly — things that take him to the borderline of self-contradiction but not quite over it. He is being contrary. It is all very complicated, but not the metaphysician's puzzle that Sartre seems to think.

He might object that I have begged the question: I chose a case where D's reason for avoiding thought is *not* that he knows thought will prove him wrong. (So I did, to show that it is possible.) But in other cases D could know this; and then he would be in bad faith. I would answer that by Sartre's own arguments we fall into an infinite regress if these other cases are bad faith; so if they exist, we must find some other explanation. Repression would do, and so (often) would what he calls 'cynicism': he dismisses this too quickly. If D's first step into bad faith is cynicism, the lie can only work if he later forgets this; but so he well might, when it is a case of drink or some other drug. ('*Why do you drink? — 'To forget that I drink.*') D might begin to drink knowing the stark truth, but knowing too that the drink will bring a muddled mind and a new mood, in which he will be able to believe what he likes. He may also sometimes begin with a simple lie (murmer 'Feeling a bit coldy' as he pours out, in rehearsal for what he will say if his wife catches him) and later, when he is muddled, bring it out sincerely — that being a phrase which (for a reason he forgets) seems right. He may also sometimes be lying from beginning to end, in which case he is never deceived at all.

We now have not just two but any number of possible explanations for what D does. Repression, wishful thinking, inarticulacy, laziness, cynicism and lying can combine endlessly to describe *without contradiction* what may look like somebody lying to himself. (And there will be more.) Sartre is doomed to make it a mystery only because he rules out so much *a priori*, when it will not fit his theory of consciousness. This includes inarticulacy: he seems to treat as basic insights for any consciousness certain thoughts that take a skill in words few people have, and none have always. But I think that he is good at picking out self-deceiving types, especially when their deception is about themselves.

To say that I am my transcendence in the mode of being a thing is not the only way to bad faith (he says) through an ambiguous 'am'. I may also claim to be, in the mode of being a thing, no more than my 'naturalistic' present state. That is, I claim to be bound by it; as Simpkin (say) might think 'I'm a drunk, I'd better accept it. No use pretending I can change'. A consciousness must know that it is not so bound; Simpkin therefore (paradoxically) lies to himself.

But why must any consciousness know this? Our freedom cannot be so very evident, if experience ever seems to deny it. And it does: ask most people if they think that all cries of pain could have been suppressed, if food can always be resisted when one is starving, if one can always choose not to faint in a crisis. If we reject this (as Sartre does) *a priori*, we must lay claim to an intuition too basic to question. And I would say that there is no such thing: even the law of non-contradiction seems basic only in that *if* we question it, *it turns out* (I think) that we cannot reason or even clearly question without it. We may certainly feel convictions too strong to withstand; we may also think in terms which it seems impracticably hard to change, at least so long as we have no proof that they are wrong. That does not guarantee them.

Without even beginning on the issue of freedom *versus*

determinism, this shows (I think) that Simpkin may honestly believe that he is not free to stop drinking. I also think that he cannot *know* that he is free in the absolute way that Sartre maintains, because this is probably false. Clinical psychology gives us data that will not easily allow even the choice in interpreting action that we usually have.

How for example could Sartre explain my hypnosis story? B is given an instruction and carries it out. '*Yet if, either before or after carrying out the suggestion, I ask him whether he is aware of any suggestion I have given him for post-hypnotic action, he will stoutly deny all knowledge of instruction*'; and why should he lie? In this case the relevant consciousness is that of the whole man B, when he is wakened from hypnosis; according to Sartre it must be translucent. But B seems to have no idea, far less intention, of opening a window when the hypnotist puts a hand in his pocket. According to Sartre it is a sign of freedom that a consciousness (and nothing else) can see its surroundings as lacking something, before acting to bring it about. But if we ask B why he opened the window, '*he will give some plausible reason*, e.g. although the air may be cool and fresh, he may say the room seemed to him stuffy and hot'. This means (if B is sincere, and again why should he not be?) that B has a *false* impression of freedom, in the form that Sartre describes. The real 'lack' is fixed by the hypnotist before B wakes: he is to see or feel or 'feel' that lack of an open window not in the room's heat, but because a hand has gone into a pocket. Everyone in the room knows this but B — at least, but BW: *some* aspect of B untranslucently recognizes the 'lack', because it is acted upon. (This is also how we know that it is the real 'lack'.)

It seems then that what feels like an intuition of freedom may not be merely inconclusive about one's motive, and therefore one's freedom of choice: it may in fact mislead. We can explain all this away only by doubting the good faith of everybody involved in such experiments, which seems far-fetched; and if we aim thereby to make Sartrean bad faith our explanation instead, it seems perverse. For bad faith is itself a paradox, by the very principles — translucency for example — that we would be trying to save.

So poor Simpkin may be right: perhaps he cannot change. On the other hand we may be slow to take his word for it. He has no hypnotist to take the responsibility: his claim must rest on what he thinks about alcoholics in general, and feels about himself. The first is speculative and the second ('introspection') may, as we have seen, mislead. He has also a motive for defeatism, which is a sad kind of wishful thinking: it is hard to try and change, and if it is also a waste of time he need not bother. But this explanation too is not a paradox.

Sartre's final pattern of bad faith also looks familiar: the man who claims to be bound by what he *is for others* — by a relationship say, or a social position, or a job. The best-known example in *Being and Nothingness*, however, seems to me to show Sartre's weak points rather than his strength.

Let us consider this waiter in a café. His movement is quick and forward, a little too precise, a little too rapid. He comes toward the patrons with a step a little too quick. He bends forward a little too eagerly; his voice, his eyes express an interest a little too solicitous for the order of the customer. Finally there he returns, trying to imitate in his walk the inflexible stiffness of some kind of automaton while carrying his tray with the recklessness of a tightrope-walker by putting it in a perpetually unstable, perpetually broken equilibrium which he perpetually re-establishes by a light movement of the arm and hand. All his behaviour seems to us a game. He applies himself to chaining his movements as if they were mechanisms . . . .. He is playing, he is amusing himself. But what is he playing? We need not watch long before we can explain it: he is playing at being a waiter in a cafe.[50]

Beautifully observed, but perhaps already a bit suspect at the point where the man's movements (as Sartre describes them) become an analogue for bad faith, as he describes that: an 'unstable equilibrium' between rival descriptions of what one is. (Compare another example, the 'flirt', whom I discuss in Chapter 8: she plays off facticity against transcendence in order to maintain 'the unstable harmony that gives the hour its charm'.)[51] It gets less and less convincing.

The child plays with his body in order to explore it, to take inventory of it; the waiter in the cafe plays with his condition in order to *realize* it. This obligation is not different from that which is imposed on all tradesmen. Their condition is wholly one of ceremony. The public demands of them that they realize it as a ceremony; there is the dance of the grocer, of the tailor, of the auctioneer, by which they endeavour to persuade their clientele that they are nothing but a grocer, an auctioneer, a tailor. A grocer who dreams is offensive to the buyer, because such a grocer is not wholly a grocer. Society demands that he limit himself to his function as a grocer, just as the soldier at attention makes himself into a soldier-thing with a direct regard that does not see at all, which is no longer meant to see, since it is the rule and not the interest of the moment which determines the point he must fix his eyes on (the sight 'fixed at ten paces'). There are indeed many precautions to imprison a man in what he is, as if we lived in perpetual fear that he might escape from it, that he might break away and suddenly elude his condition.[52]

Alienation in society is a familiar concept and can be useful, but not when it is so dramatized and over-simplified. A sentry at attention who really could not see would not be much use, for example: the 'ten paces' rule is surely (for what that is worth) based on something a little more down-to-earth than the mere ambition to turn a soldier into a soldier-thing. On the other hand a soldier at arms is indeed in some ways like an automaton. His role fixes between narrow limits the positions he may take or moves he may make; and this reflects his moral role, since military discipline can be moral alienation formal, explicit and extreme. But grocers and waiters are different: the way a waiter 'must' follow an expected pattern may be illuminatingly likened to the way a soldier 'must' obey orders, but the difference is just as important. Romanticisms like 'the dance of the grocer' and 'A grocer who dreams is offensive to the buyer' mask even more the core of truth that is here: *viz*, that the rules which define a role cannot define the individual who plays it, so that he always conceivably might refuse to play. If the waiter's movements mean that he denies this about himself, it could be self-deception. But is this likely?

What Sartre observes can be explained far more simply. Making a game of a job may just be doing what it requires more stylishly than is needed, for fun. The robot-like face and body are style: 'throwing away' an elaborate bit of tray-juggling can boost the effect, as any juggler knows. There are two ways of showing off a skill. One is to play up its difficulty: the roll of drums as the acrobat gets ready to do his backward somersault on the high wire; the other is to pretend that there is no difficulty there: the clown who five minutes later absent-mindedly does the same trick. Since acting is a skill as well as juggling, we can explain the waiter's 'eager and solicitous' act the same way. An actor may not mean to deceive even his audience (especially if he 'throws away' his lines or hams them, and the waiter does both); and if he does, he still need not deceive himself.

This passage reads to me like an unconscious echo of Diderot's *Le neveu de Rameau* (Sartre mentions Diderot once in *Being and Nothingness*, but not in connection with this). Here is a man playing toady, to compare with the waiter:

> Thereupon [Rameau's young nephew] begins to smile, to ape a man admiring, a man imploring, a man complying. His right foot forward, the left foot behind, his back arched, head erect, his glance riveted as if on someone's face, openmouthed, his arms outstretched toward some object. He waits for a command, receives it, flies like an arrow, returns. The order has been carried out; he is giving his report. He is all attention, nothing escapes him. He picks up what is dropped, places pillow or stool under feet, holds a salver, brings a chair, opens a door, shuts a window, draws curtains, keeps his eye on master and mistress. He is motionless, arms at his sides, legs parallel; he listens and tries to read faces. Then he says 'There you have my pantomime; it's about the same as the flatterer's, the courtier's, the footman's, the beggar's.[53]

Rameau's Nephew is a dialogue. The nephew is a character as well as a mouthpiece: his words are meant to be bitter, mercurial, vain and so forth. Indeed one of the nice points of the book (if one is interested in self-deception) is the way it becomes clear how far his views are shaped by his feelings, and his feelings by his situation, and perhaps his situation by his weakness. He sees every role in society as a pantomime because (he claims) society has forced on him a role he does not want. He wanted to be a great musician; he is only allowed to be the great musician's nephew. This could be false (think of the Bach family) and I suppose that it is why some readers, notably Hegel, think that the author must be identical to the disapproving *'Moi'*. And certainly *'Lui'* (Rameau's nephew) makes a more plausible self-deceiver than Sartre's waiter, on the same pattern that Sartre attributes to the waiter: he knows that he plays a part, and claims to be bound by it. Diderot's own message however strikes me as a little less simple: the fact that a man's temperament shapes his views does not at once prove them false, only suspect.

The waiter is implausible because his game does not seem to be aimed at having views. Like a child's play it is for fun, not self-deception — with certain adult peculiarities that in their turn tell rather against Sartre's diagnosis than for it. To quote Huizinga:

> The child is *making an image* of something different, something more beautiful, or more sublime, or more dangerous than what he usually *is*. One is a

Prince, or one is Daddy or a wicked witch or a tiger. The child is quite literally 'beside himself' with delight, transported beyond himself to such an extent that he almost believes he actually is such and such a thing, without, however, wholly losing consciousness of 'ordinary reality'. His representation is not so much a sham-reality as a realization in appearance: 'imagination' in the original sense of the word.[54]

To 'more beautiful, or more sublime . . .' (etc.) I would add 'funnier' and other things too, perhaps. The important point however is the difference between *imagination* and self-deception or bad faith: imagination involves feeling as if, acting as if, thinking what it would be like if, but surely (as Huizinga says) *not* coming to believe in the full sense *that* the game is truth, or trying to. The adult twist of course is that a child does not usually play at being a child (which is his role in life), or if he does, it is with an irony that he shares with adults. The waiter who plays at being a waiter is also doing a thing more typically done by someone who is not a waiter: possibly a child or a clown. In short, if what he does is not pure thoughtless high spirits and no more — if a waiter who behaves like that is making any point to himself at all — he seems to me to be reminding himself that he is *not* just a waiter, but someone who can play being a waiter for laughs.

There is nothing in Sartre's clever picture that supports or even suggests Sartre's final analysis: that the waiter is trying to throw off his inalienable human responsibility by claiming (to himself, or it would not be bad faith) that he is *nothing but* a waiter, trading as usual on an ambiguous 'to be'.

And it is precisely this person ['A Waiter'] *who I have to be* (if I am the waiter in question) and who I am not. It is not that I do not wish to be this person or that I want this person to be different. But rather there is no common measure between his being and mine. It is a 'representation' for others and for myself, which means that I can be he only in *representation*. But if I represent myself as him, I am not he; I am separated from him as the object from the subject, separated by *nothing*, but this nothing isolates me from him. I can not be he. I can only play *at being* him; that is, imagine to myself that I am he. And thereby I affect him with nothingness. In vain do I fulfill the functions of a café waiter. I can be he only in the neutralized mode, as the actor is Hamlet, by mechanically making the *typical gestures* of my state and by aiming at myself as an imaginary café waiter through these gestures taken as an 'analogue'. . . . What I attempt to realize is a being-in-itself of the café waiter, as if it were not just in my power to confer their value and their urgency upon my duties and the rights of my position, as if it were not my free choice to get up each morning at five o'clock or to remain in bed, even though it meant getting fired. As if from the very fact that I sustain this role in existence I did not transcend it on every side, as if I did not constitute myself as one *beyond* my condition. Yet there is no doubt that I *am* in a sense a café waiter — otherwise could I not just as well call myself a diplomat or a reporter? But if I am one, this can not be in the mode of being-in-itself. I am a waiter in the mode of *being what I am not*.[55]

I quote the whole passage to show how Sartre can obscure a point even as he makes it. What can the reification of 'nothing' and the empty abstraction of terms like 'neutralized mode' add to the sufficiently clear point that if *I* am said to *play a role*, I must be distinct from it? And what can they add to Sartre's further point that if the distinction is correctly made, it must class me as a Being-for-Myself, that is, a conscious being who chooses to play or not to play? (Something which, as I have said, I think that the waiter may be perfectly well aware of and may even be expressing.) And why the epigrammatic ambiguity of '*being what I am not*', when a discussion of this kind succeeds precisely to the extent that it is exact, and ambiguities are not needed?

Yet rôle-playing is a familiar form of self-deception. This is not when the aim is to amuse oneself or even (in the normal way) to do a job, but when it really does seem to force certain views on the player and these override other views that we think he must have, and should acknowledge. So a researcher into weapons might justify his work, in spite of qualms, by insisting that the duty of a scientist is simply discovery, and by identifying himself as *nothing but* a scientist:

'Once the rockets are up, who cares where they come down?
That's not my department' says Wernher von Braun.[56]

Or at least he must so identify himself where the ethics of his work are concerned. Sartre's suggestion that the player identifies himself as *nothing but* the role still looks exaggerated.

All Sartre's patterns of bad faith involve morality: the self-deceiver tries to believe that he is in some way or other not responsible. I have argued that there seems to be no reason why he should know most of the things that Sartre claims he should; but a scientist in this position knows enough to go on with. We must assume — if he deceives himself in this way — that he has certain humanitarian principles which should not let him limit himself to being *nothing but* a scientist *vis-à-vis* his work; and we assume that he knows they forbid it, and knows that he assents to these principles. He will literally (and paradoxically) deceive himself if he manages nevertheless to believe that he does not assent to them or that they allow what he is doing. If we take this possibility seriously, we may try to explain it by saying that his moral position would be clear to him if he thought it through — but in order not to face it, he does not. This only pushes the paradox a little back, so we should not take it seriously. And as in other cases, we need not: we have a large selection of other possible accounts that are not paradoxical at all, in terms of repression, lying, inarticulacy, wishful thinking, laziness and cynicism.

It is worth adding that in some cases a man might really have the limited moral principles that he claims and that we find incredible. He may for example really not see how principles apply except within a role, and see his role as something that needs no further justification. Perhaps he thinks of it as the natural one for him in his situation. If this is wrong, it will take a good deal of sophisticated argument to show why; and so it is not a basic insight which we should say a man must have. This may explain some of the most bewildering role-players: Eichmann the efficient civil servant for example, who sent trainloads of Jews away month by month to the death camps and seems to have justified this by saying that it was his job.[57] He does not seem to fit any pattern of sadist or fanatic. He had friends who were Jews, and he first supported (so, we may suppose, would have preferred) mass deportation instead of killing. Nor does he fit the label 'sociopath' or 'psychopath' who may be explained away as amoral: in some ways he seems to have been rather an over-conscientious man. The very care he took to do his job as well as he could, ignoring humanitarian regrets, suggests a strong sense of *some* duty. It may be faith or wishful thinking that leads us to suppose all people (even most people) are naturally much concerned for anybody outside their own circle. Not many are put to the test, and where experiments have been done in this line the results have not been especially reassuring.[58] And an accident of education may limit a man's knowledge about what — in his time — is thought to be one's own circle, or an acceptable moral code. In Nazi Germany

'Death camps are an unfortunate necessity' seems to have been a possible thing for a rational man to think, in the sense that it need not have contradicted anything he knew. We must hope that it was not a common one; but it goes less against the grain of common thinking at that place and time than does (for example) B's judgment that C's child was not hers, in her place and time, and I have argued that not even this is a straight self-contradiction.

Of course we may prefer to explain Eichmann as someone whose 'natural' principles were overriden by things like fear for himself or his friends, or ambition, or a compulsion to obey his leaders, or even that sadism which I ruled out *ex hypothesi* because it seems not to have been there. It may have been there, but suppressed. If so he may seem to us to have been a man lying to himself. But we can avoid that paradox if we remember the ways in which we can also explain the scientist and Mr D: cynicism, repression, inarticulacy, wishful thinking and so forth. We may also — if Sartre is wrong about absolute freedom — include a sheer compulsion to act in a certain way, which could work independently of what one knows or believes.

We do not need Sartre's tangled tale then to account either for his own examples or for others that fit his patterns of bad faith. However, what goes on in any single case may be complicated, with no one account clearly the right one. And that may begin to explain why so many people have found his theory attractive: if we instinctively expect a thing to be complex, we may accept the wrong kind of complication.

6 STRATEGY AND TACTICS

I have argued that self-deception is literally a paradox. Therefore it cannot happen. Deceptions need a split between deceiver and deceived (Chapter 2), and the only split that we may (sometimes) find in ordinary men is one that will not allow an idiomatic reflexive use (Chapter 4). If we deny, as Sartre does, that any split is possible, what goes by the name of 'self-deception' or a 'lie to oneself' will be further still from any kind of real lie, unless of course it is a real lie to somebody else. I think that splits are possible and that there is evidence for them; on the other hand, I think that we may — often if not always — find other accounts for particular cases of self-deception. These are complicated but not paradoxical; if they were paradoxical we could not accept them.

(Now that I have said that 'self-deception' literally means a paradox, some might say that I should put scare-quotes round the term wherever I use it. But we do not generally do this with figures of speech; I would rather save my quotes for times when they have some further use.)

I now want to take my discussion of possible accounts a good deal further, in order to see if they will give us any single general picture of self-deception. So far I have been handicapped by one main thing. We diagnose self-deception from behaviour; but as I have already suggested, many different ways of thinking may lead to behaviour of this kind. Any more informative story must be told as it were from inside. But if I try to report my own self-deceptions, I can speak only of the past: if I am trying now to suppress some unwelcome truth, I cannot say that this is what I am doing or I give the game away. I must rely on memory then. I have some confirmation from experience that I may (generally) trust my memory of things like this, and I know of no special reason why I should mistrust the memories I have chosen. They are of things long past, which have no power over me now, at least none that I can feel. I may also refer to other people's own stories when (again) I see no reason why these should be biassed, and to people in fiction who are seen from inside, when the writer seems to aim at psychological truth. The dangers of such sources are clear and I do not forget them. But they are the sources we have, and a good deal more than nothing.

My main example will be autobiography: a single long episode during which I tried to fend off a certain judgment that p, in the teeth of the evidence. I make 'p' singular although it involves many propositions, because they were all linked in a single story. I shall not be precise about p. It had to do with a clash of loyalties and projects, which led to a clash of roles: standard topics. Other self-deceivers may supply their own content. What I am interested in here is the *tactics* of self-deception, which may be studied to some extent independently of any content. All we need to know is that one loyalty/project/role was what I acknowledged, the other *prima facie* was not. To admit that p would have been (among other things) to acknowledge it.

I believe that my ways of not admitting that p sometimes took the form of burial or repression: p did not occur to me at all, when p was much to the point. How this happened goes of course beyond my experience, but its function in that context seems clear enough: means to an end rather than accident. On the other hand, I seem to remember times when I was in various ways aware of the proposition p. They were also times of which I might say that I refused to admit that p, even to myself — that common formula for self-deception which mere burial will not fit. But it was a complicated process. Persistently to avoid admitting that p came so close at times (I think) to persistently admitting it that I can often barely tell them apart. To *assert unequivocally* that p would have been to admit it. But I seem to remember that I explicitly *entertained the idea* that p a good deal, only I never quite allowed that it was true. I made a joke of it to myself. I said it (or part or a hint of it) ironically, to myself and sometimes to others. I was like Arnold Bennett's Mr Osmond Orgreave: ' "*Of course I know I'm an old man*" said Osmond, condescendingly rejecting [his son] Charlie's condescension. He thought he did not mean what he said; nevertheless, it was the expression of the one idea which latterly beyond all other ideas had possessed him.'[59]

I used the idea in daydreams and then dismissed it as only a daydream. I thought about it 'detachedly' as one possible, even plausible way of seeing things, which was nevertheless only one of several. At times I would even admit to myself that my obsession with p as hypothesis or daydream meant that p's possibility was important to me. In short, I thought out half-truths and lies that looked very like p and used all the words I would have used to admit that p; but they were so framed that they stopped just short of committing me.

As I argued in Chapter 1, the self-deceiver must avoid admitting not only the main topic of his self-deception, but that *he may have reason* to conclude it. He must therefore not admit that he is trying to suppress it. (See the 'self-deceiving mother' example.) But this condition too may hold more tortuously than we might expect. For example we might think that a self-deceiver cannot say to himself 'I am refusing to consider *whether* p' or '. . . *what I really think about p*'. In the cases I have so far described I did avoid saying this, since I gave my thoughts about p in an explicit turn the other way: it seemed to me that I had thought out *that p was a proposition I need not accept, on the evidence*. But at other times I did not avoid it; what I avoided was giving (to myself) my real reason for not thinking out whether, after all, p. Typically I would find some reason why now was not the right time. I even used p's importance to me as an excuse. C.S. Lewis' devil Screwtape uses the same tactic.

I once had a patient, a sound atheist, who used to read in the British Museum. One day, as he sat reading, I saw a train of thought in his mind beginning to go the wrong way. . . . Before I knew where I was I saw my twenty years' work beginning to totter. . . . I struck instantly at the part of the man which I had best under my control and suggested that it was about time he had some lunch. The Enemy presumably made the counter-suggestion that this was more important then lunch . . . for when I said 'Quite. In fact much *too* important to tackle at the end of a morning', the patient brightened up considerably; and by the time I had added 'Much better come back after lunch and go into it with a fresh mind', he was already halfway to the door. Once he was in the street the battle was won. . . . [60]

The self-deceiver may even shift the borders of the hidden country so that he can say 'I *at all times* avoid considering whether p'. He can do this by giving a false reason for never deciding *whether* p, which masks his real aim not to admit *that* p. Consider for instance: 'It is not a wife's place to question her husband about his business affairs, my dear. I leave all such things to the gentlemen'.

But I think that at other times the hidden country was laid bare. The examples that I have given so far were part of a system of behaviour that may *as a whole* be called my self-deception. The name applies dispositionally, of course: if for no other reason, I was sometimes asleep. And no doubt we could insist that the only actual self-deception was when I did not admit that p — that these times alone will allow me to use the dispositional term for the whole. But this would be to ignore other behaviour which had the same interest and intent; which, in short, served the same strategy; it therefore looks perverse to pay that behaviour no attention.

Some of it might be said either to admit that p or not, depending on how we tell the story. It seems to me that I sometimes stated that p to myself and at once recanted: 'No, no, I don't really think that!'. Perhaps I always meant to take it back; in that case the whole manoeuvre seems best described as one more tortuous way of almost, but not quite, making the forbidden judgment. Perhaps I did not; and then it seems better to say that I shifted between phases when I did and when I did not admit that p. What I do know is that I have no way (now or ever) of telling which is right. Other cases *are* admissions. My occasional burial of p seems to mark one end of a scale at whose other end I acknowledged that p to myself completely, and often did not retract it for hours. But these were hours when I was not in a position to act on my knowledge. At times I admitted this fact too, and could cynically predict that I would recant when the time came to do something about it; at other times I made desperate resolutions which in hindsight look sincere. It seems to me too that I sometimes spelled out the whole story to myself, most painfully, when I *was* in a position to act on it — and could not make myself do so. Nor could I tell anybody else what I told myself. My pain was somewhat soothed by the thought that the trap in which I seemed to be caught was very interesting (and if I did not think so still, I would not have written this). I also less plausibly thought that I must be a rather interesting person to have been caught in it.

Again Screwtape describes a case like this.

Sooner or later . . . the real nature of his new friends must become clear to him. . . . If he is a big enough fool you can get him to realize the character of the friends only when absent; their presence can be made to sweep away all criticism. If this succeeds, he can be induced to live, as I have known many humans live, for quite long periods, two parallel lives; he will not only appear to be, but actually be, a different man in each of the circles he frequents. Failing this, there is a subtler and more entertaining method. He can be made to take a positive pleasure in the perception that the two sides of his life are inconsistent. This is done by exploiting his vanity. He can be taught to enjoy kneeling beside the grocer on Sunday just because he remembers that the grocer could not possibly understand the urbane and mocking world which he inhabited on Saturday evening; and contrariwise, to enjoy the bawdy and blasphemy over the coffee with those admirable friends of his all the more because he is aware of a deeper, 'spiritual' world within him which they cannot understand. You see the idea — the worldly friends touch him on one side and the grocer on the other, and he is the complete, balanced complex man who sees round them all. Thus, while being permanently treacherous to at least two sets of people, he will feel, instead of shame, a continual undercurrent of self-satisfaction.[61]

'Undercurrent' suggests however that the patient does not admit to himself either the self-satisfaction or its reason, nor that he is being treacherous. I was sometimes more explicit.

I used another trick too which I cannot clearly place either as admitting that p or not. All that it shows is preoccupation. Besides plain jokes I made nonsense ones (some quite elaborate) that were p-inspired; I think that I knew it as I made them, or at least as soon as they were made. Furthermore nearly every verse or drawing or other such thing that I did at that time expressed (somehow) something to do with p. I worked hard to get the verses right, but they were always in metaphor. This may have been as good an explicit admission that p as any other, given how well I understood them — for I think that I understood very well indeed. On the other hand, I liked doing them, to the point of obsession, whereas literal statements were painful when I could make them at all. Clearly I was avoiding *something*. I also remember thinking quite freely about the jokes, that I seemed compelled to make them; and about the verse that (1) *I was at least getting some poems out of all this* (I did not specify what 'this' was) and (2) *writing them probably kept me going* (I did not specify where).

I believed that I wrote the verses for myself. But I nearly

always seemed compelled to show them to some of the other people concerned; and I always told the jokes to someone or other. Their symbols were easily seen through, but for various reasons this did not force p out into the open. I think that I would not have risked it if I had thought there was any danger — at least if I gambled, it was with a fair assurance. I shall come back later to the parts that other people can play in games like these.

Finally I remember a time of near escape. I could for a day or so tell the whole story clearly to myself, and nearly all of it to one of the people involved; and I could act on what I said. But other main characters in the story were not there, and I was therefore not called upon to be honest in more ways than one. When that was needed, I relapsed.

Tricks like these use words. If even words, even words (with luck) accurately remembered, may not as we look back be clearly placed, tricks without words are worse. They tend to hold less internal evidence. I remember a way of starting to think 'p' and breaking off, and another of sheering away from some thought that would naturally lead to p — wordlessly, or so it now seems. Here I can be fairly sure that I avoided admitting that p *in words*; but that is all. And we do not always need words to be aware of things in a way that amounts to admission. To adapt one of Fingarette's examples, I can 'spell out' to myself the steps of a dance or my fingering on the piano without words, simply by watching each move (visually or kinaesthetically or tactually) as I make it.

What is it then that makes such thinking an unquestionable (though wordless) admission of some truth? For a start, I think, I must not be moving habitually. Of course I *can* know that I am doing a thing when it is habitual, but I need not; so having done it, or even apparently remembering the (habitual) doing of it later, is not evidence enough. I think that I must be seen clearly to have recognized what I did, in some required way. When an admission is in words, I may show that I know a situation to be soandso by my choice of them (silent or aloud); correspondingly when I recognize it without words I may show it if I see or imagine or treat it *as* soandso, unequivocally. If it is recognizing *fingering on the piano* this seems easy: surely I could not make *those* moves correctly on *that* thing if I did not see them so? That is if I am paying attention to them at all?

I might imagine a self-deception to fit all this. I avoid paying attention to my fingering on the piano because it would force me to see how clumsy my hands are now. I am old, perhaps arthritic; I shall never play well again. We may suppose that I have to concentrate on fingering whenever I learn anything new or relearn anything that I have forgotten, or stop to correct a mistake: I now avoid learning and relearning, and if I make a mistake I ignore it. If I make it several times or anyone comments on it, I give up that piece. I must also not admit that this is what I am doing; so if ever I need to account for my behaviour to others or to myself, I find some plausible reason: too busy, out of practice, not in the mood. . . . And I may do this too without words, especially if it is to myself. I may either say in my mind (turning over a page that needs relearning) 'Oh, I can't be bothered now!' — or merely imagine myself starting to practise and feeling not stiff in the hands, but bored.

But I wrote this story to order. It is different when I have to assess my real remembered self-deceptions. Thoughts without words may be perceptions or (in my case) images that are mostly visual. In either case I remember them in images; and an image is easier even than words to interpret in more ways than one. This is true even of cases where I am sure that I watched (in some sense) what I was doing. The piano example is misleading because too good: it is so nearly psychologically impossible to play an instrument with attention if we do not know that this is what we are doing. Few things that we do are so determinate. I can watch myself push a door without seeing that I slam it, watch myself slam it without seeing that I am slamming it in your face, watch myself slam it in your face without seeing that I am doing it to annoy Grandmother, not you. . . . At times so many ways of seeing may be relevant that in all good faith I cannot pay attention to them all. I may not know whether I paid attention to a given one or not, as I look back; and if it seems that I missed it, it may be even harder to say whether I missed it in self-deception or merely by chance.

In deciding, I look beyond that remembered thought to its context, as I must also do for remembered words whose force is not obvious. But if I do this, I decide that a thought was or was not self-deception because of my overall strategy and not some one particular tactic. I am therefore not bound to insist that at some particular time in a self-deception I was aware that p, or was not; refused to admit that p, or admitted it; believed that ~p or did not. Sometimes I may be able to decide these things and sometimes not; I still have reason to say that I was deceiving myself, as self-deception is usually diagnosed.

(This seems a good time to stress again that we need not in *any* case suppose that what happens is paradoxical. When I can remember and give a clear answer 'from inside', it is always without paradox. When I cannot, it is only that the issue is not clear.)

How might I identify a doubtful tactic as self-deception? I have already suggested that we may recognize *means to an end* (Chapter 1), or *interest and intent*, or overall strategy. Going by examples we can say more: in all the cases that I have described so far, other people's as well as mine, the end, the intent, the strategy seems to involve either following or avoiding some course of action. To this extent Sartre is right, I think, when he says that a self-deceiver flees some truth about himself. We may flee truths about other things too; the truths about ourselves may even be determined by them. Demos' 'self-deceiving mother' is a case in point. But among those things which we will not accept there will typically be a description of ourselves of one particular kind: it will make certain actions necessary or impossible for us, or appropriate or inappropriate. For example: if I believe that I do not drink too much (and if I am rational) I cannot intend or resolve to give up drinking too much. It will seem not just pointless, but logically impossible. My first step if I resolve to do a thing must be coming to believe that (at least in this sense) I can. *Admitting* it — to myself, that is sincerely — is to manifest free knowledge of it and, *a fortiori*, belief; such an admission may therefore be a way of declaring intent.

An obvious way to avoid doing something, then, could be to lose, or failing that to bury, some relevant knowledge: we may then lose the relevant beliefs. And failing *that*, it seems — from my experience at least — that certain lesser ways of not admitting what (somehow) we know, may let us act inappropriately to our knowledge. The way from being aware of or admitting something — for example 'By my own standards, I drink too much' — to acting appropriately is a dark one. It involves that vexed issue, the Socratic paradox. But I think that we often behave in self-deception as though only some forms of admission were dangerous: either forcing us to act as we do not want to, or freeing us to do so, when we would rather not be free. Avoiding these, we may find 'safer' ways of saying what obsesses us irresistible: my jokes and verses for example.

I also think that no one form of admission need feel dangerous all the time. Certainly in my case it seemed to vary, which would explain my scale that runs from the burial of p to its clear assertion. It also seems to me that the closer I came to explicit assertion the more in danger — on the whole — I felt. I would let the ice get thinner and thinner beneath me and then run back to where I felt safe ('No, no — I don't really think that!').

This means/end relation between *avoiding dangerous admissions* and *avoiding action* may be an illusion. The logical relations that I mentioned, between certain admissions and certain declarations of intent, are in another category. It could be that both admission and act are determined by something else; or if we are free but (*pace* Sartre) not always so, the admission could be merely a sign that we are now free to act as we always knew we should. But in all these cases, things would look the same.

(We might find support for the means/end theory in something that Stanley Milgram says about the subject in one of his 'obedience' experiments:

Despite his numerous agitated objections, which were constant accompaniments to his actions, [the subject] unfailingly obeyed the experimenter. [That is, he went on — as he thought — giving more and more painful and perhaps dangerous shocks to a screaming 'victim'.] . . . He displayed a curious dissociation between word and action. Although at the verbal level he had resolved not to go on ['*No sir. I'm not going to kill that man! I'm not going to give him 450 volts!*'] his actions were fully in accord with the experimenter's commands. This subject did not want to shock the victim, and he found it an extremely difficult task, but *he was unable to invent a response that would free him from [the experimenter's] authority. Many subjects cannot find the specific verbal formula that would enable them to reject the role assigned to them by the experimenter.*[62]

At least it supports the *look* of such a relation.

To sum up: it seems to me that in my case some split or 'dissociation' was always there. But it was not always a split in memory or awareness; nor between one form of awareness and another; nor between awareness and the ability to speak the truth; nor being able to speak it (to myself and others) in some words but not all. These were different tactics and I used them at different times, all (I think) with one single end: to split off *what I in some way knew* from the only *appropriate action*. I might add that the aspect of p which most obsessed me, as I remember, was precisely this. Thoughts of p as hypothesis or daydream typically took the form 'what I would do or say if p . . . but I needn't'; and that whole time is coloured in my memory with a shadow of feeling compelled, of being addicted to doing and saying what the facts should have made impossible. Other feelings too seemed to help me to avoid not so much knowledge and belief, as action. I have mentioned vanity and a 'detached' interest in my own condition; there was also depression, lethargy and despair, all of which can make it hard to do anything at all, much less anything challenging. And as I cynically or despairingly noted, these states tended to be well-timed.

This fits our stock examples too, on the face of it. D will have to do something about his drinking, once he admits to it. The scientist (call him 'Dr S') must give up either his job or, given his humanitarian principles, his pretensions to morality. Mrs M must reveal that she disapproves of her son, and then must cope with hurting and being hurt by him or being openly pitied, perhaps blamed, by other people.

But another stock example of self-deception is a man I shall call 'C' for 'cancer', though any dangerous illness would do. He has symptoms that normally would be too unpleasant to ignore, he knows (or has *prima facie* good reason to believe) that they may be of cancer, he also knows that in a case like this the only intelligent way to act is to go at once to a doctor — but he does not. In the teeth of the evidence, he seems to think that nothing can be wrong. He explains away pain as some trouble with (say) his digestion, weariness and loss of weight as due to a slow recovery from flu, and so on. Certainly action is involved here: if he admits that he should go to the doctor he will probably have to, and if it turns out that he has cancer (or anything else that is bad) he will have to change his life: tell his friends and family, give up his job perhaps, act like a sick man and maybe a dying man. But here we may find it very hard to think that any of this action is the main issue. Death and pain (surely) are what C dreads; it is the knowledge that they may be in store for him (surely) that hurts him now. Should we not insist then — taking this case as a paradigm — that self-deception must after all be mainly a way to avoid the *distress* which is caused by some kinds of knowledge? And that self-deceivers typically avoid action only when it is action that will not let them forget?

Certainly our first intuition about them is that they try to avoid not painful action but painful truth. I do not think that a novelist (say) could create a convincing self-deceiver except to this pattern. The same test-by-fiction however gives an interesting, though a more complicated, result, if we use it to see how believable self-deception is that involves *no* action. Here are two cases that I have written to order. One we might more naturally call delusion than self-deception, but both raise the same issue: the delusion like the self-deception allows its subject not to face a painful truth.

Betty and Emma are paralytics. Neither can move or communicate, both can see and hear. They are both in hospital. Emma has a favourite daughter, Joan, who does not visit her. Others do, and she should know from what they say that Joan has no good reason not to come. But she will not accept that Joan does not care about her — perhaps even dislikes her now that she is ill. She tells herself 'Joan has such a busy life!' — but Joan's sister Lucy comes, and Lucy has a demanding job and a family and lives farther away. When Lucy's talk reminds her of this, Emma thinks how much more sensitive Joan has always been: Lucy would not understand how the sight of her sick mother might distress the child. It crosses her mind that to indulge such sensitivity could be called selfish, and she goes on to think 'And of course I *would* be distressed if she came and broke down — she would realize that, it would be like her!'. But Lucy brought Joan once long ago and Joan showed no sign of distress, unless leaving in a quarter of an hour may be so taken. Emma takes it so; she also holds Joan's visit to be proof that Joan visits, often forgetting that it was only once and long ago. If she remembers, she also remembers that the child was always vague about time, she was late for everything. If she ever for a while thinks 'Perhaps Joan really *doesn't* care if I live or die!' she soon takes it back, calling to mind times when Joan behaved affectionately as a child, and generalizations like 'A girl can't do without her mother, even if she does sometimes seem to take her for granted!'. And so on. Juggling these thoughts (as I did my thoughts about p) Emma avoids a mental life in which 'Joan does not love me' is an accepted truth. Its denial after all does not contradict anything that she positively knows.

Betty has escaped into her childhood. She was very ill once then, and she thinks that her illness now is the same one. She is not sure who her visitors are — she does not follow much of their talk, so tends not to listen — but she thinks of them vaguely as family. One boy, her grandson, she thinks is her elder brother. All this allows her not to know that she is an old woman paralysed by a stroke, without hope of getting better.

I find these stories believable; I would have to be or meet a recovered case of the kind to say more. But paralysis does not stop all action, only the muscular sort. We speak in imagination as well as aloud, choosing words in the same ways; we can call up mental images or dismiss them. Emma's self-deception seems to need such things. Her self-deceiving thoughts are most plausible if we think of them as imaginary conversations. She will explain in her mind to the nurses or to anyone and no one why her other daughter, who loves her, does not visit; she will invent dialogues with Lucy and with Joan, in which she writes all the parts. Betty's delusion may of course be passive, like a dream (though I think it need not be — for that matter not all dreams seem to be passive). But *ex hypothesi* it has a function: to mask a truth — otherwise it is too far from self-deception to concern us. And if Betty came to admit this truth or to believe it, it could affect intent and action even for her. If she believed in God, or in gambling on God's possibility, she could appropriately decide to pray. She could no longer appropriately plan to go to Venice next winter, and it would become impossible for her now to plan what she will do in 1920 (the year after she was ill as a child). While she escapes facing the truth, in some sense of 'face', it is still possible to see her as a kind of self-deceiver. When she can no longer do anything that counts as facing the truth rather than not, I think that all temptation to see this as a self-deception vanishes; and it was a borderline case to begin with.

We might still insist that what finally vanishes, making this no longer in any way a case of self-deception, is a necessary means, not an end: that avoiding action is tactics, not strategy. My own experience seems to belie this, since the one and only thing that the whole project always produced was unrealistic action or inaction; and all that I have heard or read of other self-deceivers fits this view at least as well as the other. But there is a further point to make. Emma and (up to a point) Betty are credible *individual* self-deceivers, because knowledge can distress us and — subjectively speaking — to avoid distress is an end in itself. But I do not think it is credible that all self-deceivers or even most should be like Betty and Emma. This is because, biologically speaking, avoiding distress is a means. We will not really understand self-deception until we have seen why what relieves such distress is useful — not (or not only) to individuals but to our species; or if not useful in itself then a by-product of something else that is useful. (It seems too much a part of human nature to be mere aberration or accident.) And from this point of view Betty's and Emma's self-deceptions cannot be typical: it makes no difference to the species' success or survival whether paralytics who will not recover feel distress or not. They are like the amputee who feels pain in a lost leg: the pain goes on when its function is lost.

What is saved when we who are not paralysed avoid distress by not facing it? *Prima facie* a kind of consistency: a view of things that fits how we want to behave and want people to treat us. Philosophy students who are not interested in ideas or argument as such may resist when one points out flaws in their arguments for God, because 'My life would have no meaning without religion', or for freedom of the will because 'This would mean the breakdown of morality'. They will not bother to resist arguments about the ontological status of numbers unless they are also studying mathematics, and it seems to make some difference to their work. Those of us who are interested in ideas or arguments as such may defend almost any apparently useless thesis to the point of self-deception; but by that stage we will almost certainly hold a vested interest in the work that we have put into it, including making it fit with other things that we accept. We probably also have interest vested in intellectual vanity; and then the topic hardly matters.

One can see how (in people if not in ants) consistent

behaviour may demand a consistent epistemological view of ourselves and the relevant world, accepted both by the agent and those he deals with. Acceptance at this level could be anything from a shared certainty that the view is true, to a shared certainty that it is false, plus a shared lie. One can also see why consistent behaviour is vital to a co-operative species. Behaviour as such presupposes (surely) certain interests; consistent behaviour presupposes a set of consistent ones. (An ant's set seems highly consistent.) When somebody's interests are too various for him to co-ordinate, he must choose some and in some way or other get rid of the rest. If this means (for us) accepting one view rather than another, it makes sense, biologically speaking, that views we find inconsistent should distress us. So we will avoid them if we can — though, like acceptance, *inconsistency* and *avoiding a view* may take various forms. And if adaptability is useful to us too, another thing makes sense: the interest or self-satisfaction that we may feel as well as pain, when two sets of interests, and their accompanying world-views, clash. Screwtape's 'patient' may have been a traitor to two sets of people; he could also live in either of two societies.

It may seem strange, if consistency is what he aims at, that the sign of a self-deceiver should be inconsistency: seeming to believe in the teeth of the evidence, showing that he (somehow) knows what he denies, by knowing so well where not to look. But if what he aims at is consistency of *behaviour*, he may be doing the best he can. We may not know what goes on in a self-deceiver's mind; but once we know what he is deceiving himself about, he is as predictable as anybody else. And if he can get us to play along, he will be able to trust us as we can trust him.

Let me end this chapter with an 'outside' view to balance my 'inside' stories. It comes from an article about cancer patients.

The subtleties and paradoxes of communicating with the patient . . . cannot be understood . . . without some insight into the gradient formed by varying degrees of hope, optimism and denial. Each may be slight or considerable and, as in normal life, may vary from day to day and from month to month. 'Denial'. . . is when a patient takes a less serious view of what is happening to him than he would do if it was happening to somebody else; 'forgets' what he has been told about his diagnosis or prognosis; or 'denies' some unpleasant possibility. . . . The doctor needs to be sensitive . . . to conflicts in the patient's mind arising from occasional or sustained use of this useful, perhaps essential, protective mechanism, which may be quite fragile (easily upset by a chance remark; a newspaper article about cancer; the death of another patient) or more deep seated. . . . Perhaps when he is with one person he seems to know; when he is with another he seems not to know. . . . Finally, a patient may show denial to such an extent that friends and relatives can scarcely credit it; and those looking after him . . . may attribute such 'lack of insight' to brain metastases.[63]

The author suggests several possible 'inside' stories very like those I suggested for Messrs C and D: 'He may know, but not want to think about it. . . . Perhaps he accepts possible death, but can still plan for recovery or remission. . . . He may have no illusions, but not want to talk about it'. He also points out that such behaviour at other times may be useful and admired: 'The ambivalent feelings we all have about these things are shown clearly when on the one hand we talk of 'wishful thinking' or 'self-deception' as if this were unhealthy or a sign of weak character; and when on the other we admire optimism and 'refusal to accept defeat' . . . as a sign of strength, resilience and courage'[64] — things of course that can help a species to survive. There is even some confirmation for my idea that the self-deceiver may see one way of putting the facts as 'dangerous' while others — coming to much the same thing — seem not to be; and that this may vary from one occasion to another, in this case from patient to patient. It seems that some patients will accept that they have cancer but 'deny' a bad prognosis; others will accept a bad prognosis, but only if the word 'cancer' is not used. Sometimes this may simply be due to ignorance: the patient believes that 'cancer' always means something horrible and incurable. At other times it seems more like a taboo.

It is revealing that even doctors who are most anxious to use the word cancer initially in the interest of 'complete honesty' will seldom use it subsequently, unless the patient particularly seems to want this, which few do. . . . Many patients find that if they use the word too freely their friends are embarrassed and avoid them. McIntosh observed during prolonged observation of patients with cancer in hospital that most of those who 'knew' or 'probably knew' preferred to use euphemisms when talking to each other.[65]

I have said that I think a description of ourselves or something that affects us may frighten us because we feel that if we accept it, we will have to act appropriately. A sick man could feel such fear (like pain in a missing leg) when its link with all effective action had gone; paralysed Emma might avoid a word like 'cancer' in her thoughts. But using a taboo word *in public* is unquestionably an act. For the patients described here it seems to be the act of suggesting that their disease is not only serious but 'shameful and hopeless' and setting themselves (perhaps) to behave accordingly. They may be able to bear acting like people who are gravely ill, and they may know that their illness is cancer and know that their friends know it too; but to avoid that final act of embarrassment they seem to prefer sometimes to be taken for self-deceivers. It may be worth it if, in doing so, they can arrange how their visitors are to behave.

7   A CHANGE OF MAP?

Given what I have said so far, I might be expected to approve of
the line taken by Herbert Fingarette in his book *Self-
Deception*.[66] To some extent I do, but I have many reservations.
Fingarette suggests that accounts like Demos' fail because
'Paradoxes arise in connection with self-deception when we
characterize it primarily in terms of belief and knowledge, or in
terms of "perception" language such as "appear" and "see"
. . . . We might initially and loosely call this entire collection the
"cognition-perception" family'.[67] He suggests a remedy.

I do not propose that we eliminate the 'cognition-perception' family . . . from
the analysis of self-deception. I do, however, propose a fundamental shift of
emphasis . . . divorcing certain of the 'cognition-perception' terms from that
family and showing, by reinterpretation, that they would be better treated for
our purposes as members of the 'volition-action' family. The terms to be thus
split off are 'conscious' and the variants built on this root.[68]

The shift is from a passive model for consciousness to that of a
skill, and from a 'weak' sense of 'conscious' (on the first model)
to a 'strong' one.

The specific skill I particularly have in mind as a model for being explicitly
conscious of something is . . . the (learned) skill of 'spelling out' some feature
of the world. . . . Sometimes — but by no means always — the 'model' activity
(literally making something explicit in language) is also an instance of the skill
(becoming conscious) for which it serves as a model. However it is clear that
one often becomes explicitly conscious of or . . . spells-out something, without any evident utterance, even to oneself, or with only allusive or cryptic
ones.[69]

I take this to mean that not all making explicit in language is
'spelling-out' and not all 'spelling-out' is making explicit in
language. We are given no other definition of wordless
spelling-out, only examples: the main one is 'spelling-out my
fingering on the violin'. To become explicitly conscious of
something is to spell-out some way in which one is 'engaged in
the world'.

It is logically necessary that it should be typical of an individual's engagement in the world that the description be cast in terms of such categories as aims, reasons, motives, attitudes and feelings, of understanding and 'perception' of the world and himself. What a person does not somehow take account of is not part of his engagement in the world.[70]

That last sentence gives a strong enough sense to 'engagement' only (I think) if we take it to entail 'Anything that a person *does* somehow take account of *is* part of his engagement in the world'. Then we must define 'take account of' and 'person' so as to avoid the same kind of ambiguity. Fingarette later makes an important distinction between 'person' and 'individual':

Insofar as I refer to identity as constituted by avowal [that is, the avowal of *'identifying oneself to oneself as a certain person, or as a person engaged in the world in certain ways'*] I shall speak of *personal* identity or, simply, of the *person*. Insofar as I refer to identity without implying the avowal of that identity as such, I shall speak of the individual identity or, simply, of the individual.[71]

In the earlier passage the terms seem interchangeable, but in which sense? I think that for both we should read 'individual'. If 'engagement' is not to beg questions, we should be able to identify its subject in the plainest possible way: by his body. We can then distinguish the ways in which a man engages himself in the world *as a certain person* from any other engagements which the individual has, but the person does not avow: this is crucial for Fingarette's thesis. I think too that we should count any reaction at all to a thing as somehow taking account of it; for we shall also need to distinguish between what someone takes account of but does not spell-out and what he takes account of by spelling it out. We seem to have no way of recognizing the first, if not by the rule that I suggest. If I so much as flick off a fly in my sleep, I somehow take account of it; and the fly is thereby a part of my engagement in the world. (Obviously it is not a part that I spell-out.)

The immediately crucial point is that we are not in general explicitly conscious of our engagements in the world. . . . We must see explicit consciousness as the further exercise of a specific skill [which] requires sizing up the situation . . . to assess whether there is adequate reason for spelling-out the engagement. . . . We are also assessing the situation to see whether there is reason *not* to spell-out . . . .. These are presumably weighed against one another by the individual. Whether or not he spells-out the matter in question, or exactly how he does so . . . will depend not only on his assessment but also on his ingenuity in adapting to the conflicting conditions.[72]

Spelling-out and refraining are themselves both ways in which we are engaged in the world; so we may also spell-out *that we are or are not spelling-out a thing* — though we do this only if there is some reason for it. The way to self-deception is now clear: *'There is over-riding reason not to spell-out the engagement, [and] we skilfully take account of this and systematically avoid spelling [it] out . . . [we also] refrain from spelling-out this exercise in our skill in spelling-out. . . . A policy of this kind tends to generate a more or less elaborate 'cover-story'.*[73] The person uses the skills involved in spelling-out to cover the gaps that will appear in his normal occasional spellings-out, whenever he gets too close to the hidden engagement. He will try to make this 'cover-story' as consistent as possible, and as close to fact as he can get it.

If we describe self-deception in this way we can certainly avoid some kinds of paradox. We will not fall into Sartre's regress ('To put myself into bad faith I must be in bad faith already'). We can also avoid the Hylas/Philonous issue if we understand 'engagement' and 'take account of' in the way that I suggest. Fingarette's *engagements that are spelled-out* and *engagements that are not spelled-out* seem on the face of it to be concepts that we know how to use: at least we can often recognize spelling-out as he describes it, and we can learn about an individual's engagements in the world from what he does and says. We can also (often) know when spelling-out would be appropriate; and it seems right to stress the importance in self-deception of policy, a consistent cover-story, volition and action.

This is not enough however. Consider my own self-deception. Some of the things that I did (including burying knowledge) are quite well described as avoiding spelling-out that p, p being in my case the engagement in the world that I tried not to face. Other things clearly are not: the times when I told myself the whole story without acting on it. And of a wide middle ground it seems impossible to say whether 'spelling-out' applies or not. This is especially clear when we remember that we can spell-out without words (Fingarette is surely right about this) or 'with only allusive or cryptic ones': did my jokes and verses, in which I said allusively what I would not say literally, avoid spelling-out that p or simply spell it out in another way? And why, by Fingarette's account, should one way seem better to me than another?

I could certainly stretch and cut my story to fit the 'spelling-out' theory of self-deception. I could say that the tactic of spelling-out that p but not acting on it had indeed to some extent the same policy as my self-deception, but that it was not self-deception itself; I could say of all cases in doubt that either I did avoid spelling-out that p, or else I was not (quite) deceiving myself. But we could justify such trimming, I think, only if Fingarette's analysis (like no other) could give us a sense of 'self-deception' that is literal and without paradox. No 'volition-action' account can do this, and Fingarette's has problems of its own.

He says that his aim is 'to draw a new map of the region, rather than to correct details in the familiar sort of map', at the same time trying 'to produce enought detail on specific checkpoints to make it evident that the map does correspond in its main outline with the terrain'.[74] Now a contour map (say) may be more use at times than a map that shows only towns and roads. But it will not make the road-map false so long as the roads exist. Fingarette commonly writes as though his kind of map will elminate the other. When he says 'I do not propose that we eliminate the 'cognition-perception' family of terms from the analysis of self-deception', this seems to refer only to a few terms like 'conscious' and 'sincere'. He thinks that we can recast these as mainly action-volition terms. 'Know' and 'believe', on the other hand, bring paradox into any literal account, and so we must wipe them off the map. But this is impossible: as long as self-deceivers are people, 'know' and 'believe' must apply to them somehow. And if the only ways in which they can apply all make literal self-deception into a paradox, it does not matter what other maps we have and how useful: we cannot take 'self-deception' literally.

Anyway how can a map of self-deception that leaves out knowledge and belief be literal? See Chapter 2: literal self-deception must be deception, and I defy anyone to define 'deceive' without involving them. 'Deceive' has an action-volition side too of course (A *keeps B from* knowing or *makes* B believe) but it tells only half the story. Fingarette does not seem to see this.

Rather than . . . persisting in such questions as 'Does he *really* know?'. . . we should ask instead, 'How is he engaged in the world,' and 'Does he express this engagement explicitly?' . . . Why are 'know' and 'believe' used in the everyday idiom . . .? Because the crux of the affair . . . lies in the area demarcated by the phrase 'becoming explicitly conscious of', and because consciousness has traditionally been characterized in the language and imagery of knowing, believing and perceiving. There are many contexts in which . . . such language and imagery are useful. [But] . . . if we wish to put matters directly and non-paradoxically instead of indirectly and paradoxically, we must turn to this largely unexplored way of characterizing consciousness.[75]

He judges 'know' and 'believe' as we judge metaphors, for their usefulness in pointing towards the truth rather than their correctness in stating it; and if 'indirect' does not mean a figure of speech — as opposed to his own 'direct' account which is literal — I cannot think what it means.

In fact his own account breaks down at exactly those points where he should bring in belief and knowledge, but does not. Take for example a key passage in the third chapter, where he sets out to recast 'sincere': the paradox of the self-deceiver's 'insincere sincerity' rests (he says) on an ambiguity. 'Sincere' in its usual sense means that (1) *an individual is in some way engaged in the world and is not unintentionally wrong about his engagement;* (2) *he purposely tells himself the truth about his engagement;* (3) *he tells other people the same as he tells himself.* But (2) is not essential: the main point is (3).

[In self-deception the person] gives himself the very same story he gives us, [and so] we initially characterise him as sincere. Yet the more we observe him, the more we . . . come to see that the story he is telling both himself and us is . . . purposely wrong. . . . We are puzzled by this because we have failed to think of explicit consciousness as a form of telling something.[76]

But consider Richard Hannay, about to elude the agents of the Black Stone by impersonating Alexander Turnbull, a roadman:

I remember an old scout in Rhodesia, who had done many queer things in his day, once telling me that the secret of playing a part was to think yourself into it. You could never keep it up, he said, unless you could manage to convince yourself that you were *it*. So I shut off all other thoughts and switched them on to the road-mending. I thought of the little white cottage as my home. I recalled the years I had spent herding on Leithan Water. I made my mind dwell lovingly on sleep in a box-bed and a bottle of cheap whisky. . . . On I went, trundling my loads of stone, with the heavy step of a professional. . . . I was already counting the hours till evening should put a limit to Mr Turnbull's monotonous toil.[77]

Hannay can change his story when he needs to: 'Then a herd passed by with sheep, and disturbed me somewhat by asking loudly 'What had become o' Specky [Mr Turnbull]?'

'In bed wi' the colic', I replied, and the herd passed on' — but so may a self-deceiver change his cover story, as Fingarette is right to suggest. Hannay recognizes the agents when they arrive and understands their German asides to each other; but he does not tell himself this, so he is still not clearly marked off from the self-deceiver. Finally he stops telling himself the roadman story when he drops the disguise; but so might a self-deceiver drop his cover story, along with his self-deception. But what Hannay means by 'convince yourself' is not what Fingarette means by 'sincere'. We would do better to say that Hannay *imagines* being sincere, in order to act his part better.

The point is quite general: if an act may be sincere, it may also be play-acted. Speech acts are no different, not even mental ones like telling oneself a story — that is while we describe them in purely action-volition terms. To call a man sincere is indeed to say that what he says matches something else, but this cannot be another act of saying: the second could match the first by being insincere too, making *him* insincere in the pair of them. Volition gives no more of a criterion than action, since both actors and self-deceivers tell their false stories on purpose. (I mean that both acts have a motive.) The deciding point, in short, lies beyond the action-volition range. Surely I am sincere insofar as I *believe* the story that I tell, never mind to whom I tell it; and I have argued in Chapter 2 that 'believe' must be epistemological (that is, a 'cognition-perception' term) in such contexts.

If this is true of 'sincere' it will be true for 'cover-story', since a sort of sincerity is what distinguishes the cover-story from Hannay's imagining. We shall also need 'sincere' in its more usual sense to distinguish spelling-out from both of these. Indeed if we do not feel bound to avoid 'know' and 'believe', the simplest way to describe spelling-out might be to say that it is how I think of an engagement — without words or with them — when I know that it is mine, and when my knowledge is actual (that is, not just a disposition) and free (that is, it entails belief).

Without all this, Fingarette's terms are unusably vague. But he is right to fear that it will force us back to a choice between paradox and metaphor. The self-deceiver (A) is engaged in the world somehow. He assesses this fact (p) and finds over-riding reason not to spell it out. Either this engagement-plus-assessment-plus-decision operates entirely without consciousness (Hylas' story) or it does not. If it does, both 'self' and 'deceive' become figurative in 'self-deception' (see Chapters 2–4). If it does not, A will be *somehow* conscious of the engagement (etc.), or a part of it. If he is conscious of too slight a part to give the game away, the situation is as before; and if he is conscious of something that *would* give the game away we may treat this as though he were conscious of p itself; for his awareness of *that* will now be a topic for self-deception. (It will be like p* in the 'self-deceiving mother' example.) If he is conscious that p, he can only be so in the 'weak' sense, by Fingarette's account. And this is not a paradox; but it fits more states than self-deception. His over-riding reason not to spell-out might for example be acute laziness when it comes to spelling-out anything, unless he really has to. He becomes clearly a self-deceiver only when (by normal standards) he would have to spell out that p and still avoids it, hiding the 'gaps' with a cover story.

Telling oneself a cover story must be to become explicitly conscious of some false engagement in the world, contrary to the real one: A avoids spelling-out that p by 'spelling-out' what is or entails ~p. But 'strong' or 'explicit' consciousness, as Fingarette defines it, is not believable if it does not include the 'weak' kind of consciousness too: I cannot make something explicit to myself without *being aware* that this is what I make explicit. So A is aware of something contrary to p in the story he tells himself. Still no paradox; but we have seen that this fits not just A but Richard Hannay. We must add that A is aware of his story *as his belief*: that is, he believes something contrary to p. It must moreover be *clearly* contrary to p, or it will not make a cover story. But *ex hypothesi* he is also aware of p as the truth. If A is not split, this means that A knows freely that p; and then belief in p's clear contrary will not be possible. We must therefore assume a split, and in fact Fingarette himself posits one later, for other reasons. But this makes his account no more 'directly' self-deception than many others.

This does not mean that I think we should abandon the 'spelling-out' theory entirely. The distinction between explicit and inexplicit consciousness seems useful even if we cannot always be sure how to apply it in particular cases; and once we have put back the cognition-perception element, *avoiding spelling-out an engagement in the world* seems to describe very well a good many of the self-deceiver's tactics, even if by no means all.

After he has said how he thinks self-deception happens, Fingarette goes on (as I did in Chapter 6) to consider why. I suggested that it might be to save a certain consistency of behaviour, as best someone can who is addicted to an unrealistic course of action. Fingarette says that it exists to save personal identity; and he defines that term in an unusual way which at certain points brings his thesis close to mine.Other key terms are *'individual'* (defined by contrast to 'person', in a way I have already quoted), *'avow'* and *'disavow'*.

The person is defined by those engagements in the world which he avows. We avow engagements by spelling-out (so avowal need not be in words). Not surprisingly, 'avow' in this special sense turns out to be no more clearly defined than 'spell-out': we are told instead its alleged role — determining personal identity— and that the public use of 'avow' *'is related to* [*this one*] *and is a model for it'*. [78] Otherwise we are told only that it is 'an 'inner act', which is to say it is not in the ordinary sense an act at all, for we can never say of any peice of overt conduct that it *is* the act of avowal'. [79] But I think that it is not an act in *any* mere 'action-volition' sense. To be avowal rather than a cover-story it must be sincere, which raises the Hannay issue. (My own improved definition of 'spell-out' would get us round that.)

The person is also said to be the part that *dis*avows. But given the spelling-out theory, this seems inconsistent. If a self-deceiver disavows an engagement in the world by not letting it become explicitly conscious, it must be the individual (surely) that assesses whether it is to be avowed; then in avoiding avowal the individual disavows it *for* the person. If a person's identity consists of all that he *does* avow, then anything that precedes or prevents avowal and is not itself avowed must lie outside. If anything is made explicit it will be a cover story. Fingarette however treats disavowal as the avowal that one is *not* somehow engaged in the world; and both kinds of avowal take the form of a description of oneself, though it may be put obliquely.

A father announces: 'You are not my son. From henceforth I disown you' . . .
Taken as the disavowal of identification which the second sentence reveals it
to be, the first sentence can be lived up to or not — but it is not false. . . .
[The] assumption necessary for my thesis is that something significantly
analogous . . . is commonly done in the privacy of one's own soul.[80]

At first sight 'You are not my son' looks performative here,
and so necessarily public: we do not have social or legal systems
in the privacy of our souls. If not public, this must indeed be an
analogy. But we often use performative-sounding words to
make resolves (no doubt we hope to bind ourselves psychologically by what might at other times bind us socially). Resolves
may be made to other people, but they also *must* always be made
to ourselves if they are sincere. I see no need then to bring in any
such analogy: avowal and disavowal look like the kind of self-
description discussed in Chapter 6. They identify certain acts as
impossible for us or possible, inappropriate or appropriate; and
in doing so they declare intent.

This is where my thesis touches Fingarette's. But he would
go on to say that the descriptions primarily identify us as certain
persons: the acts' appropriateness (etc.) follow from this. 'The
crux of the matter is this: certain forms of spelling out are in
their implication clear affirmation by a person of his personal
identity. One who disavows an emotion, an intent, a deed
thereby surrenders the authority to speak as one who feels,
intends or does so and so.'[81]

A person so defined turns out to be a type rather than a
particular. This need not affect Fingarette's thesis about self-
deception, but it is interesting *qua* theory of personal identity.
We have not the mind or soul here that metaphysicians have
looked for: a mental substance which, being a particular, is
unique. And the body identifies not the person but the individual. The *person*'s 'body' is different.

Even with regard to something as 'concrete' and 'objective' as the body, it is
interesting to note that *my* body as I identify it for myself is what the
psychiatrist calls a 'body image' . . . just because he sees that it reflects, in
effect, my engagement in the world . . . rather than the object the disinterested observer would describe.[82]

Suppose that the fairies replaced your body by a changeling's
exactly like it. If they then gave the changeling a mind exactly

like yours (including memories of course) he would not know that any change had been made; but still two individuals would have been switched. It is not clear that two persons would have been. He would identify himself to himself as the person that *you* were; and Fingarette seems to hold that such identification is definitive. Since you (the individual) would also identify yourself to yourself as that person with equal authority, it seems to follow that two individuals can be the same person. You and the changeling would become — that is, instantiate — different persons only when and if you (in Fairyland) and he (on Earth) began to avow different engagements again.

One might object that when the changeling identifies himself to himself as you, he is avowing *false* engagements: his 'memories' for example are not real memories. Since he is deluded about what his real engagements are, he must be wrong about the personal identity they establish. But when the changeling sincerely says 'I have never been to Fairyland' the statement is false only in that his body has been there; and the body identifies only the individual. *Qua* person he has not been there, until he has avowed the appropriate engagements in the world.

Multiple personality seems to depend on a distinction very like this, though perhaps not identical to it. When Eve Black says of Eve White 'I know her thoughts like she knows them herself. I don't think them of course', her 'I' cannot refer to Eve the individual, nor can her 'she'. If they did, 'I don't think her thoughts' would be nonsense. If for the sake of argument we forget the fairies, we may perhaps safely treat the instantiation of any one person as unique; but the two Eves suggest that they still need not be in a one-to-one relation with individuals.

A baby, Fingarette says, is not yet a person. A child becomes one, but for some time he can 'pursue specific engagements independently, as autonomous projects, without integration into the complex unity of a personal self'.[83] And it sometimes happens that an adult individual is drawn into

. . . a kind of engagement which, in part or in whole, the person cannot avow as *his* engagement, for to avow it would apparently lead to such disruptive, distressing consequences as to be unmanageably destructive to . . . that currently achieved synthesis of engagements which is the person. . . . 'Self-deception', [Freudian] 'defence' and [Sartrean] *'mauvaise foi'* [are names for] 'regressions' to [the child's form] of engagement; they manifest our capacity for such isolated engagements even after the emergence of a personal self, and in spite of the unacceptability to the person.[84]

I find some of this intuitively plausible, but most of it impossible to prove one way or another. It seems fairly clear that we begin as mere individuals and only later grow into anything like persons in the Fingarette sense. But to call self-deception 'regression' suggests that it is not part of the normal adult equipment; and it is so common that this is surely unlikely. If we say that it is part of the adult *individual's* equipment but not the adult *person's*, this begs the question. Fingarette's key terms, too, seem definable only in a circle. The person is a synthesis of avowed engagements in the world; to avow an engagement is for the person to make it his own. We avow by spelling-out, and to spell-out an engagement is to become explicitly conscious of it. What is explicit consciousness? The exercise of a skill: spelling-out. We cannot further define spelling-out, unless we go back to avowal. 'Watching' or concentration may be necessary to it but are not sufficient, because we may concentrate on an engagement in some of its aspects and leave out others. Words are neither sufficient nor necessary: we have lies (*inter alia*) on the one hand, and 'spelling-out my fingering on the violin' on the other.

This is no doubt why Fingarette makes so much use of 'models' — that is, of analogy; but arguments, and therefore theories, based on analogy have an inherent weakness (see Chapter 2). And it is not only that the analogy may always fail us at the crux: it may also be right in a way that we do not see, so that we draw the wrong conclusions. I think that some of Fingarette's most important ones are like this. For example 'spell out' in common usage is a model for his 'spell-out'. But when we spell out a thing for someone in the ordinary sense, we must first understand it ourselves; we then succeed only if we make *him* understand. This involves cognition — and so, surely, does spelling-out in Fingarette's sense *in fact*; but he does not see it.

I have suggested that 'free and actual knowledge' might be a way to define 'explicit consciousness'. 'Know' is not reducible to action and volition terms; but philosophers since Heraclitus have suggested that it demands a skill. If so, action and volition are involved. Traditionally this skill has been called the use of judgment or recognition or understanding, and some structure like that of language has been assigned to it: this would fit spelling-out. Free knowledge entails belief; and to judge that a thing is true is to come to believe it, at least in the epistemological sense. To recognize or understand that a thing is true is again to come to believe it, *because it is so*: come to know freely, in fact. This breaks Fingarette's closed circle of terms. And I might define 'know' adequately for what we need here, I think, in terms of *truth*, and *having learned*, and *being in principle able to remember*. But to distinguish between free and buried knowledge we need 'believe'; and I think that is different, unless we define it merely in terms of emotion and behaviour, which will not give the epistemological sense. We can get no closer to a definition, I suspect, than to give near synonyms, each with its own irreducible epistemological element: 'accept', 'assent privately' and so on. Or we can follow Fingarette and give 'models'; but models do not define. Still 'believe' is a term that we all seem to need, and manage to use successfully, in spite of having (I think) to treat one main aspect of it as primitive.

But if we break out of the circle like this, we can no longer both define 'person' as the synthesis of an individual's avowed engagements in the world and equate avowal with spelling-out. In my own experience the self-deceiver avoids a *kind* of avowal perhaps, and a kind of damage to himself as a person or to his avowed engagements in the world; but he does this in many more ways than failing to spell-out. What he *consistently* avoids is some course of action; so if this is also in any sense self-destruction it must be the destruction of himself as the player of certain roles, rather than the speller-out of certain engagements.

The destruction of some of the person's roles, the redescription of himself in a way that seems to demand a change of action: we must ask finally why these should always be seen by the person as *self*-destruction. Fingarette's thesis here seems to me both too dramatic and too simple. An engagement in the world may be both unrealistic and addictive, and still not feel like part of his essence to the person concerned, so that he is afraid of disintegration if he gives it up. No doubt he may be afraid of this at times; but it may also be enough sometimes that a present convenient habit of life will be lost. To insist that any engagement in the world which is important enough for self-deception *must* be essential to the person, or to define 'person' in a way that makes this necessary, is again to beg the question.

From the ways that we describe people (including ourselves) and from the way that I think of myself, it seems to me that different types identify themselves to themselves in different ways. I do not mean philosophers' theories of personal identity here but (as Fingarette does) our working rule: how we think of ourselves. Abnormally dissociated 'selves' illustrate this in their own way. For some reason or other they cannot (as the rest of us think we can) see their body as all their own, and to that extent a condition of identity; and what they go by instead seems to vary widely. There is the 'self' marked off purely by emotion, action and attitude: Eve Black, B of BCA, A too for a time (but it did not last). On the other hand there is A later and there is Eve White, both split off most obviously by cognition: unconscious of B's and Eve Black's past or present consciousness. This was of course not deliberate, but nevertheless it seems clearly related to their characters. A and Eve White were each the one of her pair that had a strong conscience and a conventional way of thinking: they might not have been able to dissociate themselves as B and EB could from any acts or feelings which they could remember 'from inside'. Or consider R.D. Laing's patient, 'James', who felt compelled (so he said) to act as 'his mother's puppet':

He had developed his subjectivity inwardly without daring to give it any objective expression. In his case this was not total, since he could express his 'true' self very clearly and forcibly in *words* [at least to Laing]. . . . There was, however, hardly anything else 'he' did, for all his other actions were ruled not by his will, but by an alien will, which had formed itself within his being.[85]

'James" criteria do not seem even to add up to a personality: cognition, a few selected tastes and feelings, no action at all to speak of except (sometimes) speech.

More usual people seem to vary in a like way. We go by our bodies more, of course; but our most popular fantasies and religions show that we often do not think of our bodies as essential. And, bodies apart, some of us speak as if we defined ourselves mainly in terms of what we do; others by what we do when this involves other people, perhaps certain other people especially, or by how other people seem to react to us; others by one main role or vocation or intellectual position ('artist'; 'nun'); others by how we perceive, experience, remember. Think of Proust's *À la recherche du temps perdu, versus* Lord Baden-Powell's *Lessons from the 'Varsity of Life*.[86] Even day-dreams, which most of us discount, may seem to some people to be at the centre and real life at the edge, or at least no more essential:

> The mature work of Charlotte and Emily [Brontë] cannot fully be understood without some knowledge of the play-sagas of their childhood, and by the violent, long-drawn, uninhibited daydream life to which they gave rise. . . . Charlotte in maturity recognized the dangers of the dream and consciously broke out of it . . . .. Emily stayed resolutely within it. . . . and by doing so achieved freedom for the development of her genius; an unself-conscious masculine freedom which in real life her difficult temperament might never have allowed.[87]

Or we may select an essential self from some combination of these, or of others among our engagements in the world. It need not mean that we disown the rest; we may only think of the rest as more dispensable, like the man in the *New Yorker* cartoon who says 'Statistical analysis is what I DO, not where I'm AT'.

An Existentialist might say that any such ordering of engagements is bad faith. And it would be bad faith certainly to treat an engagement as though it were not there; but surely it is bad faith too to pretend that it is either more or less central to our feeling of who or what we are than in fact it is. My self-deceiving scientist for example could not say 'Research into biological warfare is what I do, not where I'm at' without bad faith: the issue involves him too far. I have made him aware of this in my example. His disavowal is a different one: 'Any kind of research can be where a scientist is at, and I am essentially a scientist. What others may do with my results is their own affair'. This is to make certain moral principles seem less essential to him than (*ex hypothesi*) they are. Nevertheless I see him as a man who does also identify himself strongly as a scientist. And if he is afraid that giving way to his disavowed moral principles threatens *that*, he may very well be a full-scale Fingarettean self-deceiver, who feels that his identity is at risk.

We may, I think, disavow an engagement in the world for fear of something less: no more than the loss of our identity's skin or a few outer leaves. Here I go back to my own experience of self-deception: one thing that I remember clearly — it was one of the compensations — is a heightened feeling of *myself* through it all, going on whatever happened. When I could think about it explicitly I saw the mess that I was in and the coming crash as a failure of will, action, loyalty and so forth; but, *pace* Fingarette, I thought of it always as *my* failure, not the failure of myself. In a way I felt more myself because I could not (or possibly would not) talk about it: I did not have to mould the truth into other people's terms. And when the crash came, it seemed that I had been right about this: it brought guilt, anguish, confusion, helplessness, relationships and plans upset; it gave me a new picture of myself in many ways, more complicated and less flattering than my old one; but I think that it never changed my basic way of identifying myself to myself.

This was luck: my identity's skin and outer layers might have been differently placed — even at the core — in a different person. I had (I think) happened to identify myself always first in terms of perception, memory, imagination, understanding, rather than as an agent or by what I was to anybody else. And again luckily (since these last two things must still be important, unless one is a 'James') my roles and loyalties clashed, but neither one by itself was too unlike my idea of myself as agent. It might have been different if I had found myself torturing cats.

This leaves me with more of an action-volition account than Fingarette's is really. I would like to keep his description of self-deception as *disavowing an engagement in the world*, typically by avowing a cover-story. But if I do so, I must redefine these terms so that action (or avoiding action) becomes the main issue, and the fear of losing one's personal identity becomes only one way in which that issue may appear to us. Fingarette says that we must ask *why* self-deception happens as well as *how*, if we are to understand it; but his answer 'To save personal identity' needs the same treatment. Insofar as he gives any answer to that, it seems the wrong kind: 'Without this, man would be at most a highly co-ordinated, even highly intelligent animal, engaged in a sequence of pursuits in entire and inevitable unself-consciousness. Such creatures might be numbered or named, and even referred to as 'persons', but they would not have the capacity for the moral or spiritual life'.[88] Perhaps so.

('Moral' no doubt; but 'spiritual', given how often the *loss* of personal identity is taken to be that life's goal?) And we may indeed have reached a point *now* where these things are ends in themselves for us, just as avoiding distress or pain is. But I can still ask why we should have reached it, or more directly, why *being a person* should have become valuable to us. Why are we not, why do we seem determined not to be, the unself-conscious animals that Fingarette describes? If I believed in a God who valued personal or moral lives I would answer differently; as it is I suggest that consistency of action is again the likeliest answer. (This involves morality, by the way: no specific morality necessarily, but the disposition to follow a code.) And Fingarette's stress on the *integration* of engagements for a person suggests the same: in fact his theory of self-deception seems to entail mine, though mine does not entail his.

He sees his theory as a branch of the psychoanalytic tree. His final description of person and non-person in self-deception is of two ego-structures: the Ego and a 'counter-ego nucleus' which is conscious but not explicitly so. This is a Philonous story, as opposed to the classic psychoanalytic Hylas story. He also distinguishes it from recent developments in psychoanalysis which try to avoid the issue of cognition altogether, stressing the 'dynamic' side of defence.[89] And he is surely right not to follow these: no theory which ignores the cognitive side of self-deception can cope, for example, with the Richard Hannay problem. Therapists may not need to do so; epistemologists must try.

But his own theory will not cope with the Hannay problem either, until we build more epistemology into it than he wants. And when we have done this, we can very rarely be sure that a person (or Ego) is not spelling-out its disavowed engagement *somehow*; moreover, even when we are sure — when it seems to be buried for instance — we still cannot choose betweeen Philonous and Hylas when it comes to explaining it.

The Freudian schema which he follows leads him (I think) to make another mistake.

The rudimentary character of the counter-ego nuclei, their isolation from the civilising influence of the Ego, and the consequent lessening of concern with strict logical, causal, temporal and highly rational relationships, make counter-ego nuclei much cruder, more 'primitive', in the form of their expression. They are indeed 'closer' to the id insofar as the latter constitutes the uncivilised, highly unspecified basic drives.[90]

Freud's own theory of defense may presuppose that any live but disavowed engagement must be infantile; and no doubt many are. But if we look at self-deceivers with attention, I think it becomes clear that many are not. For example, a man may disavow that assessment of a state of affairs which is by normal standards the only rational one, because it would tell him that he probably has cancer. His avowed assessment by contrast may try to look consistent, but manage only the silliest kinds of sophistry. Again, the expression of a disavowed engagement, as opposed to its content, may be 'primitive' — obsessional acts that seem senseless, clownish Freudian slips and the like — but it need not: I have given examples that suggest a much wider and subtler range. Between the sillier kind of cover-story and (say) a carefully-worked poem that puts the 'counter-ego's' case clearly in metaphor, which is the more primitive?

The moral status of a disavowed engagement is therefore more complicated too than Fingarette allows. An adult self-deceiver often seems to disavow his *better* self, which grew up avowed and civilised. Dr S for example tries to suppress the conviction that his work is wrong — wrong on humanitarian grounds which may not be the only possible standard, but which are adult almost by definition. Since they may not be the only possible standard, the conclusion that he suppresses is not necessarily right; but only serious moral enquiry can justify any other. Dr S may indeed try to suppress it *because* he once spelled-out a better case for it than any he can now spell-out for its rival: 'A scientist's only duty is to research'. If so, his knowledge of how the argument went must be disavowed along with its conclusion, or his policy is not self-covering. All this suggests that any guilt which he disavows may not be 'id-like' either, but rationally based and subtle in its direction. It will probably not belong to the whole disavowed engagement: he is likelier to feel obscurely proud of that side which I have called his 'better self'. (Compare Screwtape's 'continual undercurrent of self-satisfaction'.) He will no doubt feel (and disavow) guilt for having disavowed it; and for the second-rate standards that have won out; and for anything else that ignobly explains why they have won: ambition perhaps, or a fear of insecurity or of being thought a crank.

There is a final point. Fingarette's theory requires a split self-deceiver: the person or Ego *versus* that other side whose engagement(s) must not be avowed. I have suggested that although he says it is the person who disavows the engagement, it would be better to say that the individual does so *for* the person. But his own way of putting it may now seem easier to understand, for the individual's ban on spelling-out depends in turn on certain engagements which *ex hypothesi* the person has already avowed. Since the new engagement is incompatible with these, the person must when he avowed them have disavowed engagements of the new one's general kind, at least by implication.

But the engagement *whose disavowal is his self-deception* is not just any engagement of the kind, it is this one, the one that the individual now has. To disavow *it*, the person would have to acknowledge somehow that it is there to disavow; and this is usually exactly what he must avoid. It still seems better then to say that the 'deceiver' is some part of the individual which is not the person; the person's earlier avowals will be the individual's over-riding reason not to spell-out.

That is, if he does not spell-out. I say that a self-deceiver may do so completely; and even more often he seems to spell-out in a few 'safe' ways while avoiding others. He may also shift with great versatility from one such mode of disavowal to another. This gives me one more reason to complicate Fingarette's picture of *the person under threat* on the one hand, and *an isolated 'counter-ego nucleus'* on the other. If I am right, the boundary between Ego and Counter-Ego is neither so clear nor so stable as he suggests. This may in turn explain why the (variously) disavowed engagement need not be infantile in content or expression. Fingarette's 'Counter-Ego' is *ex hypothesi* inarticulate, or nearly so: its engagements are never spelled-out. But if the split can shift along the scale that I have suggested, so that the only thing always dissociated is some course of action, then they *can* be spelled-out. Whether they are or are not, and when, will depend on what the self-deceiver is like. And even if they are never spelled-out as an assertion of the truth, they may be — I suspect that characteristically they will be — *entertained* explicitly as hypothesis or daydream, very often to the point of obsession. And when we can entertain an idea hypothetically, we can reason about it.

8 SELF-DECEIVERS AND OTHER PEOPLE

IF self-deception works as I think, it is often a lie only to other people. The self-deceiver (A) is very well aware of the truth that he is trying to deny, but he acts as though he were not — except that he may seem to know where not to look. Why then do we not see him as a liar? Here is A professing that ~p, when ~p is obviously false, and we have reason to think that A knows it is false. Lying (or if it is not in words, pretending) is surely the simplest explanation, and it is a thing that we understand: there is no paradox about a lie. It cannot be A's apparent sincerity that puts us off: any competent liar professes that.

I think the reason is that for all his apparent sincerity, A seems so very far from competent. '*A pretends that p is false when we are sure that he knows it is true*' will fit a liar; but we usually want to add that A must know that *we* know p is true, and that we know that *he* knows. Mrs M's friends no doubt saw through her nasty son long ago and (however tactfully) have let her see it. Mr D's wife tells him to his face that he is drinking a lot nowadays, and she bases what she says on what she has seen him doing; he could not ask for better grounds. And so on. How can they hope to get away with it? So we may wonder if they can be lying after all.

But this could be to miss the point. A cannot hope to persuade us that p is false, perhaps, or even that he lacks reason to know this. But what if he hopes to persuade us — since after all we cannot see into his mind — that in spite of everything *he believes that p is false* (or sometimes: *he does not know that it is not*)? If p is very evident this may of course mean that he is trying to make us think he is out of his mind. And if he does not otherwise seem to be so, probably he will not persuade us easily: why should we credit him with a belief that is absurd? But this doubles back: perhaps we should. How could any man who was not at least a little mad, at least on this one topic, expect us to swallow such a story? And if he were not a little mad, why should he want to make us think that he is?

But if we therefore cannot believe that A is lying, we forget that what he may dread above everything else is *having to admit* to us that p. To do so may commit him to action which he cannot face; it may also lead us to treat him in ways that he cannot bear. So long as we waver between 'He can't believe that!' and 'He does!', A is safe, even if only for a little while; and if p is really obvious, this may be his only resource. As a last resort it may be enough if he makes us think not that he *does* not know that p, but that he *may* not; or if he leaves us not sure what to think.

Whatever the effect, he is lying. Normally we hold people responsible for lies. But in a case like this, even if we finally decide that A is lying, we may still not know what to think: so desperate a pretence could be beyond the liar's control. He may not even *want* to pretend. We may therefore not know how to judge him morally, and we almost certainly will not be sure how we should treat him. While we hesitate, he gains more time.

A may have another motive too, which I have already mentioned. He may feel (like Mr D) that the literal statement of his case does not give a fair picture. His lie is a symbol for what he thinks is the *real* truth which (for many possible reasons) he cannot or will not tell us more clearly. It seems to D that he is *really* a moderate drinker. He has reasons why, although they are weak. He drops the 'really' when he speaks to his wife: she ought (he feels) to understand. If what he actually says sounds implausible, all the more reason for her not to take it literally. A lie so motivated will also of course gain time, and D may be playing for that as well, and may be aware of it.

There is also the constructive lie. Another favourite example among writers about self-deception — and surely a good one — is a husband who 'believes' in the teeth of a good deal of suspicious behaviour that his wife is faithful to him: if she were somebody else's wife he would suspect her at once. And he may indeed believe what he seems to: all the tactics of self-deception are open to him, including the burial of evidence. But he may simply hope that if he goes on *seeming* not to know the truth, his wife will come to her senses. Mrs M too may feel that if she (alone of all the world) did not seem to respect him, her son would go completely to ruin. And she could be right: we can lie to people about themselves with perfect success if they are at all suggestible. But to do so we may need to look sincere in the teeth of such overwhelming evidence that other people think we are lying to ourselves. Typically however when we lie in this way it is also *about* ourselves, I think (as Sartre says); but not in bad faith, simply as means to an end. D for instance may feel that he will stop drinking in time if he gets no worse, and that he will get no worse if he is limited by having to pretend. (He may of course feel other things that I have already suggested as well; more often than not a lie like this, I think, has more than a single motive. But he need not.) Or there is the mood-changing lie. I feel afraid, for instance; so (like the lady in the song) I strike a careless pose, whistle a happy tune and do other things that may look ungenuine to the sensitive observer. I hope to fool people however, and if they are not too observant I may. But notoriously

> The result of this deception
> Is very strange to tell,
> For when I fool
> The people I fool
> I fool myself as well

— which I shall now translate: I do not fool myself, I change myself (if the trick works). And if this is what I hoped would happen, it may have been my lie's main aim: for if I can change myself, I shall not need to fool other people for long. The change has worked when I no longer feel any fear; and there need be no paradoxical stage between that and my first state, one in which I fool *myself*. Either I go straight from *feeling afraid and pretending (to others) that I do not* to *honestly not feeling afraid*, or I go through a halfway stage that is different. Like the woman walking through a graveyard I may know, by certain symptoms, that I will feel afraid (again) unless I distract myself. I distract myself in this case by going on with the act, pretending now not that I do not feel afraid, but that I do not even feel the risk of it.

Lies to change ourselves often fail. When they are about more than a mood they may often be almost bound to fail, and the liar may know it. C (the sick man) has perhaps read of miraculous cancer cures worked by the invalid's indomitable will to live. He knows that even if such things happen they must be very rare, but he cannot afford not to try. He must (he thinks) therefore never give in to illness; and admitting that he is ill would (he feels) be giving in. So he pretends not to be ill — not to fool himself and die, but to change himself and live. He sees his lie as a gamble. Wishful thinking may help him, but not even wishful thinking is necessary. His friends, looking for some more commonplace motive, cannot understand why he should be lying; they conclude that the poor man must be self-deceived.

He may of course also be self-deceived another way, since he may pretend from more motives than he knows openly. The 'gamble' might indeed be a cover-story for something simpler: he is addicted to his usual life, the life of a well man. At some level he — the individual, not the person — is determined at all costs to hang on just a little longer. Lies at one end of the scale, buried knowledge at the other, and all (non-paradoxical) degrees between may always be mixed in a self-deception, whenever more than one proposition is at issue. Still if C's friends think that he somehow does not know *that he is ill, probably with cancer* they will be wrong in this case: about that he is only lying.

When death is close enough to seem more terrible than illness C may admit that the gamble has failed. Then suddenly he may stop publicly pretending. Emily Brontë's death fits this pattern, as Charlotte Brontë records it.

Emily's cough and cold are very obstinate. I fear she has pain in her chest. . . . Her reserved nature occasions me great uneasiness of mind. It is useless to question her; you get no answers. It is still more useless to suggest remedies; they are never adopted. . . .

I would fain hope that Emily is a little better this evening, but it is difficult to ascertain this. . . . To put any questions, offer any aid, is to annoy; she will not yield a step before pain or sickness unless forced; not one of her ordinary avocations will she renounce. You must look on and see her do what she is not fit to do, and not say a word.

. . . She is *very* ill. . . . A more hollow, wasted, pallid aspect I have not beheld. The deep tight cough continues; the breathing after the least exertion is a rapid pant; and these symptoms are accompanied by pains in the chest and side. Her pulse, the only time she allowed it to be felt, was found to beat 115 per minute. In this state she resolutely refuses to see a doctor; she will give no explanation of her feelings, she will scarcely allow her feelings to be alluded to. Our position is, and has been for some weeks, exquisitely painful.

. . . She sank rapidly. She made haste to leave us. Yet, while physically she perished, mentally she grew stronger than we had yet known her. . . . The spirit was inexorable to the flesh; from the trembling hand, the unnerved limbs, the faded eyes, the same service was exacted as they had rendered in health. To stand by and witness this, and not dare to remonstrate, was a pain no words can render.[91]

The Brontës' biographer Margaret Lane thinks that Emily was trying to will herself well:

Ruthlessly self-sufficient, incapable of opening her heart or confessing a weakness, she fought her illness with the most dangerous weapon she could find. . . . Mind, according to her experience, had almost limitless authority. . . . It could create a world in which she moved at ease; induce an exaltation as passionate as love; now it should conjure sickness out of sight.[92]

But two hours before she died, Emily admitted that she was ill.

She arose and dressed herself as usual, making many a pause, but doing everything for herself, and even endeavouring to take up her employment of sewing. . . . The morning drew on to noon. Emily was worse: she could only whisper in gasps. When it was too late, she said to Charlotte, 'If you will send for a doctor, I will see him now'. About two o'clock she died.[93]

It is not clear that her sisters ever saw Emily's attitude as self-deception. But this may be because such stubbornness was in character, and they knew her well. C's friends might not know him so well; or he might never have given any sign in health that he would react to illness in this way.

When a hope like C's is very ill-founded, we may call it superstition. Superstitions may be acted on entirely without belief; and they may lead to lies or pretences that look even more incompetent than other constructive lies. For example in Mary McCarthy's novel *The Group*, Gus tells Polly that he wants to end their affair. In theory he could change his mind and come for dinner as usual, but she is practically certain that he will not. 'But if she did not buy food, this said she knew Gus would not come tonight. And she did not know it; she refused to. To know was to let fate see that she accepted it; if she accepted it, she could not live for another minute'.[94] Fingarette might say that to accept it would be to avow the engagement '*I have lost Gus*' and that this will mean Polly's disintegration as the person she now is: 'She could not live another minute'. On the other hand, she does not seem to treat acceptance as the avowal of an existing fact, or even one that perhaps exists. To accept looks performative: it is to *make* the thing *come* true, by not resisting or objecting when fate proposes it. 'She refused to know' seems to relate to something like this: (1) Polly can make a thing inevitable or not: she influences fate. (2) She does this by accepting or rejecting what fate offers. (3) To accept is to behave as if the thing will happen. When she does anything (like buying food for only one) which says in *this* sense that she knows it will, fate will fix things so that she knows for sure.

If this is a cover-story for self-deception, it is a very strange one. Polly is a modern young woman. She went to Vassar when rationality was in fashion. I do not think that we *can* take her to believe it literally, with the kind of sincerity that a real cover-story would need. We might assign a belief in fate (whom Polly can influence) to some 'primitive' Counter-Ego, but this is not what the author suggests. She suggests that Polly's thought is explicit. It seems to be saying in an 'allusive or cryptic' way that *Polly hates what has happened so much that she cannot bring herself to act as if it were true*. The story that she tells herself is certainly childish: children are always pretending that they can influence fate ('If I can count to a thousand while I hold my breath, something will happen so I needn't go to school'). But as I recall it, even children usually think in these terms without believing them, unless something happens unexpectedly to make it seem that a particular spell has worked.

I find Mary McCarthy's Polly completely plausible. I think that what happens in cases like hers is this. She is helpless and she knows it. (Children too are very helpless and they know it.) It is a kind of relief merely to *play* at doing something effective. We may play such games in self-indulgence; more often (I suspect) we feel a shamefaced compulsion, in the teeth of what we know to be true and of what people would say if they found us out. If we can be said to believe in them at all, it will be in an emotional and behavioural sense of 'believe', with perhaps at its core the cognitive belief that after all it is not *impossible*. And most of us, I suspect, do not think that other people can be as childish as we are; for that matter even children may often not suspect that other children play the same games. I have met many adults who admit that they played them as children, including people who were children when I was a child; I never remember a child telling me about them at the time, or when I was a child telling any child or adult about mine. — Here is Polly then, buying food for two. A friend who knew about Gus might well say 'Polly is deceiving herself', because he or she never thinks to say 'Polly is acting out a story about influencing fate, because she wishes that the truth were false and knows that there is nothing she can really do to change it'.

One reason, in short, that we may diagnose a lie to oneself is that we forget how many other different kinds of lie a person might tell. Here is yet another example: we may pretend to pretend. A man abuses his wife extravagantly at parties. It is an act, a joke — their friends all know it well. They may know it well enough to guess that it is not entirely an act. But it may seem so far-fetched a way to pretend *not* to abuse her really — the *prima facie* lie — that they say it must be self-deception: he cannot admit to himself what his real feelings are. And indeed he may not: when he thinks about his 'joking' he may bury any memory of sincerity. But he need not. He could know that he means most or all of what he says, either symbolically or literally, and still play the act out because he cannot help it; he could also know and be able not to play, but play because he likes to. He could act the same way in all three cases; and because it nonplusses people and leads them to suspect self-deception, in all three cases he could get away with it.

This is different again from the face-saving lie, which everybody knows to be false. Normally we would not call such a lie a self-deception, except perhaps as part of the lie. But one of Sartre's best-known examples of 'bad faith' seems in fact to be such a lie; so perhaps it needs some comment. A woman goes out with a man for the first time. She knows his intentions very well, and knows that sooner or later she must make up her mind about them. But for the moment:

. . . she concerns herself only with what is respectful and discreet in the attitude of her companion. She does not apprehend [his] conduct as an attempt to achieve what we call 'the first approach'. . . . If he says to her, 'I find you so attractive!' she disarms this phrase of its sexual background; she attaches to the conversation and to the behaviour of the speaker [only their] immediate meanings, which she imagines as objective qualities. The man . . . appears to her sincere and respectful as the table is round or square. . . . This is because she does not quite know what she wants. She is profoundly aware of the desire which she inspires, but the desire cruel and naked would humiliate and horrify her. Yet she would find no charm in a respect which would be only respect. . . . But then suppose he takes her hand. . . . To leave the hand there is to consent in herself to flirt, to engage herself. To withdraw it is to break the troubled and unstable harmony which gives the hour its charm. . . . We know what happens next; the young woman leaves her hand there, but she *does not notice* that she is leaving it. She does not notice because it happens by chance that at this moment she is all intellect. She draws her companion up to the most lofty regions of sentimental speculation; she speaks of Life, of her life, she shows herself in her essential aspect — a personality, a consciousness. And during this time . . . the hand rests inert between the warm hands of her companion — neither consenting nor resisting — a thing.[95]

Sartre diagnoses a conceptual slide between facticity and transcendence.

She has disarmed the actions of her companion by reducing them to being only what they are. . . . But she permits herself to enjoy his desire, to the extent that she will apprehend it as not being what it is, will recognize its transcendence. Finally while sensing profoundly the presence of her own body . . . she realizes herself as *not being* her own body, and she contemplates it as though from above as a passive object to which events can *happen* but which can neither provoke them nor avoid them because all its possibilities are outside of it. What unity do we find in these various aspects of bad faith? It is a certain art of forming contradictory concepts which unite in themselves both an idea and the negation of that idea. The basic concept which is thus engendered, utilizes the double property of the human being, who is at once a *facticity* and a *transcendence* . . . [Bad faith] must affirm facticity as *being* transcendence and transcendence as *being* facticity, in such a way that at the instant when a person apprehends the one, he can find himself abruptly faced with the other.[96]

A sledge-hammer to a butterfly. *Not being her body* is a good name for the game that she plays, but why think it more than a game? She might in a rare case really believe that her body is not her own, like Laing's 'James'. She might more often really not be sure about the man, especially if she is very young or he comes from a different culture. (It looks like an approach, but suppose it is only conventional for him to suggest this? What a fool she would look if she seemed to take it seriously! Best wait and see.) But usually she must know what he is after, and mean what she is doing. As Sartre says, she plays for time. Perhaps she is not yet sure what she wants; perhaps she is, but does not want to show it. She thinks yes, but not yet; or no, but doesn't want to spoil the evening. She may be stringing him along for fun, she may be looking for a chance to let him down gently — and so on. She may feel that she plays from choice; or she may feel compelled to. In any case the game looks ritualistic: as Sartre says, we know what happens next.

Sartre does not seem to notice, however, that the ritual dictates the man's part as well as the woman's. He must use language that the woman can officially disarm, however clear it may be in fact. He must let her get away with the hand routine, though few pretences could be less convincing. The people we call self-deceivers tend to worry us by their perversity; these two worry nobody, unless it is Sartre. Their game is so obviously useful. I have already given several reasons why she might play; he in turn plays presumably because if she had to say yes or no now, she might say *no* out of caution when she would have said *yes*, given time. They are also of a society which tells its women not to say yes too soon ('*Il faut se faire valoir*'); both will tend to value her accordingly. And when she 'shows herself in her essential aspect — a personality, a consciousness' her aim is probably the same: she is not denying (to herself or to him) that she is her body, but reminding him that she is a person. He as well may choose to play and may enjoy the game: some people claim to enjoy the pursuit more than anything else. Or he too may feel impatient or trapped and wish that he could break out of the pattern.

Conversations like this are common enough when people need to come to an understanding without first admitting what they want. If we like playing them (beyond what is normal in a game of skill) it may be for a reason that looks superficially like Sartre's but is really different: they let us act out ambivalent feelings. In this example both her behaviour and his, and his words too, are two-sided: hence that 'troubled and unstable harmony'. Or more widely, they may let us act out feelings without explicitly admitting to anyone that we have them. But so long as each player freely knows what the game is, there need be no bad faith. She need not in fact even deceive *him*. At most she will keep him guessing within a narrow range; but for all that she may care, he could have guessed right from the start. What matters is that he go on playing by the conventions: then she knows where she is with him, and can cope.

This makes such a game's function the same as self-deception's, if I am right about self-deception. The pattern too is very roughly the same: she acts as though she did not know the obvious. She might indeed call it self-deception later as an excuse: 'Oh, I knew what he was after really, I suppose. But he made himself so agreeable, and I needed a friend . . .' We could even say that it is self-deception which she pretends, instead of near-imbecility, anaesthesia of the hand, or abstraction to the point of madness. I would rather say that she need not pretend anything definite: all that she wants is to inhibit some acts of his, encourage others, and save face on both sides. Nobody has to *believe* her.

Sartre misses another point here, though he makes it often elsewhere (in *Huis clos* for example, as well as *Being and Nothingness*). People who pretend not to know the obvious — including 'real' self-deceivers, the ones who trouble us — are typically either playing a game with other people or trying to. If I am right about self-deception, we might put it this way: typically they have either made an unspoken treaty with other people (who therefore play along with them in some unrealistic action) or they hope to. If the other people play, it may be by choice and for many different reasons, including a wish for peace, or to be kind; or they may be caught in the same trap. Take the self-deceiving man whose wife is unfaithful. She may have every reason to know that he 'must' know it, and we would expect her to wonder at his blindness and go warily. Instead she may act recklessly, saying 'Nonsense, I *know* he doesn't suspect!' to friends who are sure that he must: why will she not see it? She must be deceiving herself, perhaps because she really hopes that he will find her out. . . . Husband and wife meanwhile, knowing each other well, compound a life day by day in which the truth from either would shock like a betrayal. The difference between this example and Sartre's is that here nobody knows (looking on) how much each is aware of, what is buried, what is compulsive, what is chosen. They do not know it of each other; from moment to moment they may not know it of themselves. And if they know, they may not be able to talk about it.

That is perhaps the only unlikely thing about the Shakespeare sonnet which is the frontispiece to this book: he says more than I think he should usually be able to say, if he were really in the state that he describes. But from my own experience, it seems that self-deceivers may have clear moments in which we can spell out our lying condition; and he is not speaking directly to his partner in the game.

Self-deception may be a conspiracy; it may also be tyranny. Emily Brontë's refusal to admit that she was ill may not have deceived her family, but it made them helpless: 'You must look on and see her do what she is not fit to do, and not say a word.' Emily being Emily, Charlotte accounts for her behaviour in action-volition terms: 'The spirit was inexorable to the flesh'; but more commonly we would wonder how much the inexorable pretender really knows, and how far he believes in his own actions. Our uncertainty about this may indeed make us even more helpless in resisting: if we cannot guess what his state of mind may be, who knows what subtle balance we will not upset if we force him to admit the truth?

Uncertainty is the crux. Except in Sartre's example and its kind, we do not know if people are pretending or not. This is not because 'there can be no false coins without real ones': of course we can pretend a thing that never really happens. (If that were not so, no father could ever pretend to be Santa Claus.) It is because we know from experience that repression does happen, and so does delusion. There is also suggestibility. As Hans Christian Andersen tells it, 'The Emperor's New Clothes' is only about lying;[97] but quite possibly some people in the crowd would really see the Emperor in clothes, especially if they are too far away to see clearly. More might later come to think that they did, or would have thought so if the child had not pointed out at the time that the Emperor had nothing on. So legends grow (flying saucers? angels at Mons?) and with them yet another kind of lie, that may look like self-deception, but is in fact (I think) no more than gullibility, wishful thinking and misplaced good intentions. 'So many people seem to have seen it that this wonderful (or salutary or heart-warming or dramatic) thing *must* have happened. Therefore (to please, to be interesting, to convince unbelievers) I might as well say I saw it too.'

To sum up: any particular self-deception could, some or all of the time, be mere pretence, so far as some or all of the lookers-on can tell. I suspect that the kinds of pretence are endless. I have given only a few suggestions. But it will seem an inept and eccentric pretence by ordinary standards; and even if we suspect that it is one, we cannot be quite sure. This is because the lie (if it is one) is not — or not essentially — about anything that we can check. It is about the liar's state of mind, including his (cognitive) belief; and believers and pretenders may look exactly alike. So can those who pretend from compulsion and would perhaps like not to, and those who pretend from choice: if he does not mind being branded a self-deceiver, a deliberate liar may get away with a lot.

9 THE JUDGE AND THE SOCIAL WORKER

I have said what I think self-deception is and (roughly) why we do it. This does not yet explain why we should give it that name: why a paradox — which therefore cannot literally fit — should seem a better description than anything else. It may puzzle us to the point of making us think that the term is, after all, 'too good a metaphor to be metaphor'.[98] But a description may seem right for other reasons than literal fit.

I think that we typically use the term (and the concept) without thinking or caring whether it is literal or not — certainly without working out that it is a paradox. But whether we know that it is one or not, we choose the term for its *suggestion* of paradox: its ambivalence matches what we feel about self-deceivers. We use it for a family of cases with this (typically) in common: it is impossible either to settle or to ignore the question 'Can A help what he is doing?'. (I mean settle the question by whatever standards we normally use. Philosophers ask it in a different sense about action in general, but that is another thing which typically we do not think out.) And the trouble is not really that only one description fits — that is, literal self-deception, which is a paradox; it is that too many descriptions might fit, and we cannot have it all ways. No single one of them is a paradox; but we do not know which to prefer, and their implications clash. We do not even know which to prefer when (in hindsight) we try to judge ourselves: for once we have seen that our motives can twist our memories, we cannot claim special first-person authority. At any rate we cannot, so long as the self-deception at issue still affects us; and even when it no longer does so, we may not remember enough (see chapter 6).

But often when judgment is hardest we are forced to judge, because we need to act. The self-deceiver himself, for example, may in a clear spell get out of his trap or not, depending on what he decides is happening. He may go to someone who can help him, if he decides that he cannot do it alone. Other people will want to decide things like: should we let him get away with this? If not, how do we stop him? Can we treat him as entirely responsible? *What is going on in his mind?*

To label him *a self-deceiver* settles some of the practical problems at least. Let me illustrate this with an unnaturally simple case, where we have only two rival diagnoses: forgetting (or repressing) and pretending. If it seems unlikely, this does not matter. Real cases are only more complicated.

John Doe and Joe Bloggs are friends who share a house. Doe sees Bloggs go out one evening; later he hears movement upstairs in Bloggs' room. He is a timid man and there have been burglaries lately. Although his memory is usually very good *Doe forgets that Joe Bloggs is out*. He therefore treats a noise in Bloggs' room as nothing to worry about. When Bloggs comes in, Doe remembers seeing him leave. He cannot think how he forgot. He tells Bloggs the whole story: it is the best he can do to explain why he let Bloggs' room be burgled.

Bloggs may agree that it is possible. As a simple case of forgetfulness it may surprise him, since John Doe is not usually so vague. But he cannot disprove it: people do forget things unexpectedly. And if he is sophisticated enough to think in terms of memory repressed, he will not even be surprised, knowing John Doe: the man's timidity will explain it.

It will however just as well explain why Doe may be lying. Suppose he had known that it must be a burglar, and dared not move from his chair: he would now be afraid to tell this to an angry Joe Bloggs. And so unless Bloggs is very charitable or very cynical he will feel torn: if he accepts Doe's story he may be letting Doe get away with an act of cowardice and a lie, at his expense; if he rejects it he must (it seems) call Doe a liar. That would be unfair: Doe's story fits all the evidence that there is. Furthermore, even if he were lying, calling him a liar to his face would antagonize him, and they are friends and share a house. Bloggs would therefore like another story that will (1) be acceptable to John Doe; (2) save Bloggs from feeling that Doe is perhaps getting away with an injury to Bloggs, and a lie; (3) save Bloggs from seeming uncharitable.

Now think of Doe. His position is shaky and he knows it. If he is to explain his lapse of memory at all, it must be in terms of fear and repression: he was afraid to face a burglar, or even leave his chair to call the police. Even if he had no control over what happened and would have avoided it if he could, it happened because he is what he is. He could not blame anybody else in his position and so has no reason to blame himself; but almost certainly he will feel vaguely guilty and definitely ashamed. He has also lost his authority to say what really went on in his mind when Bloggs was gone; for if it is granted that his memory failed him before, he must grant that it could do so now: he is still under pressure. He really cannot be sure that he *did* forget. And so he too may be ready to accept a different story, if it will (4) disarm Bloggs' suspicions of him; (5) account for his feeling that it was somehow his fault and let him offer amends (he cannot do so now without making Bloggs still more suspicious or — if Bloggs accepts both his story of forgetting *and* the amends — making Bloggs seem unfair); (6) not contradict anything that he feels sure of.

It will make things much easier if he can say 'I'm sorry, Joe — I suppose I must have deceived myself'. Bloggs can then give and Doe take some blame without either of them feeling that this is unfair: we always blame deceit unless its motive is good. Cowardice is not, and both will agree that if Doe has a motive for 'forgetting', this was it. Doe can then offer and Bloggs take amends: (2) and (4). But if Doe is to blame as a (self-) deceiver he is also to be pitied as a dupe: (3). If Doe takes some blame and offers amends, his most obnoxious reason for lying to Bloggs is gone: (5); and see (7) below. Finally if Doe successfully deceived himself he must have been deceived, which is reassuring if he is still not sure what really happened: (6); and from (4), (5) and (6), (1).

There are other benefits. (7) Joe Bloggs may still suspect that Doe is lying. But in this case it looks like a different kind of lie. Doe no longer seems to be trying to shirk responsibility at Bloggs' expense. What it seems he cannot face (if he is lying) is admitting that he knowingly did Bloggs an injury. This is clearly because he does not want to lose Bloggs' goodwill; and if Bloggs thinks that Doe cares about his goodwill, Doe is likely to keep it, especially since Bloggs has nothing to lose now in saving Doe's face. (8) Doe may still feel fairly sure that he did not deceive himself, whatever that may mean: he forgot. (I assume that neither Doe nor Bloggs would think that self-deception simply is such forgetting). Still he will not want such a thing to happen again. Some unknown side of him seems to have caused it, that is if he accepts that it was due to fear. He will probably think of this 'deceiver' as unconscious; but whatever he thinks, such things can feel like a joker playing tricks. And this much is clear: the joker is sensitive to John Doe's experience. So perhaps it may be taught a lesson: let John Doe face at least some of what this cowardly side of him 'meant' him to escape, and maybe (Doe may vaguely feel) that will be the end of such tricks. The same kind of thinking may make Bloggs decide that even if 'self-deception' is the wrong description, it is a useful one; taking everything into consideration, maybe the only useful one there is.

If John Doe and Joe Bloggs do not think in terms of *motivated* forgetting, both are likelier still to agree that it was self-deception. 'I forgot' may begin to sound unlikely even to Doe, and the strain on Bloggs' trust will be huge. Nevertheless it will seem to Doe that in spite of everything he did *not* remember that Bloggs was out; and if he sticks to that, Bloggs cannot deny it without trouble.

One might object that we blame people for forgetting: will that not satisfy them? The answer is: it might, if this were the kind of forgetting that we blame. But that is omission: something which the forgetter might have avoided if he had taken care. In this case Doe could not have foreseen that he would forget as he did; if Bloggs blames him in effect for being careless, he is bound to resent it. Anyway Bloggs will not much want to blame him for that. Avoiding a burglar is cowardice, on the face of it, and Doe is a coward by nature rather than a forgetter. The logic of 'self-deception' may not be clear; but if Bloggs wants to blame Doe for cowardice without calling him a liar, this is his only way.

The opposite simple case is the one where Doe does not forget. He is sure that there is a burglar upstairs and is too scared to move, and later he does not dare to tell this to Bloggs. Bloggs himself will be in the same state of mind as before; and if Doe is a good liar, he will try to find the story that Bloggs will like best. We have seen that 'self-deception' is that story. But Doe may choose it even is he is not a good liar. I think that bad lying is due mainly to two things: a weak imagination and the liar's frustrated honesty. Both can make him waver at the edge of the truth. If Doe pleads self-deception, he can admit at least that he must *somehow* have know that Bloggs was out; is *somehow* responsible; and is guilty of lying to *someone*, though he says that it is to himself.

These are cartoon cases, especially the first. I chose them for their simplicity. Here surely we might least expect to find problems of diagnosis, and here already they seem intrinsic. Real cases are much worse. They tend to go on longer and to cover more topics and occasions, and the behaviour that we judge may seem to run back and forward through all stages of sincerity and furtiveness, good sense and perversity, shading at last into madness. We will probably stop calling someone of the kind a self-deceiver and call him mad only when the line that he takes is too strange, his action too extreme for us to feel that after all it may be bluff. In fact a madman may bluff too: when one has a reputation for madness it must be useful at times to act madly when one need not. (A madman may do any of the things that we would usually call self-deception: see my example in Chapter 1.) But we may not think of this, as almost inevitably we think of it when somebody we consider sane 'must' know a thing and acts as though he did not. We may also feel less torn when it comes to deciding whether we are to hold him responsible: it is easier to give someone with a reputation for madness the benefit of the doubt.

I have if anything understated the problem. To say that we cannot settle whether an apparently sane self-deceiver is responsible *by whatever standards we normally use* suggests that we have some (fairly) coherent standards, whether or not they are philosophically justified. In fact we have a muddle. 'Common sense' and common usage do I think suggest a general line: neither total Existentialist responsibility nor a total determinism which makes responsibility an empty concept. Christianity for example has tended to stress 'freewill', and parents seem to assume it, and the law assumes it *prima facie*; it seems that we need it to justify punishment, which it seems that we cannot do without. On the other hand, 'He can't help himself' is (often) also a perfectly respectable thing to say.

The trouble is that it is typically a charitable thing to say. If there are any paradigm acts of which most people would agree that the agent 'can't help himself', they are too special to be of much use: a wounded man's scream perhaps as they lift him on to the stretcher (and still he may feel responsible if it tells the enemy where they are); an act done in madness (but that is not always excused: see below); acts done in terror or exhaustion (but there are heroes and saints — not everyone succumbs). On the other hand, for an act to be widely accepted as *free* without any question, it would probably have to be (1) not irrational (we often take irrationality to be a sign of compulsion), (2) not the *only* rational thing that can be done in the circumstances, (3) not something that the agent wants more than anything else, (4) not something that he does not want, (5) not something that clearly goes against his interests (which may include altruism). William Golding spells out in *Free Fall* what I think is the common, usually unspelled out, idea, with the further fairly common idea that free acts *feel* free.

Free-will cannot be debated but only experienced, like a colour or the taste of potatoes. I remember one such experience. I was very small and I was sitting on the stone surround of the pool and fountain in the park. There was bright sunlight, banks of red and blue flowers, green lawn. There was no guilt but only the plash and splatter of the fountain at the centre. I had bathed and drunk and now I was sitting on the warm stone edge placidly considering what I should do next. The gravelled paths of the park radiated from me: and all at once I was overcome by a new knowledge. I could take whichever I would of these paths. There was nothing to draw me down one rather than the other. I danced down one for joy in the taste of potatoes. I was free. I had chosen.[99]

There is nothing here to shake a determinist: that taste of freedom relates only to constraints that we also 'taste', those in (1) – (5) above for example. But, more to the point, since 'common sense' is not determinist, too few acts are like this in enough ways at once. Almost everything that is morally interesting or important seems to lie between what uncertain paradigms we may accept for freedom and compulsion, and so we seem almost always to have both a hard line and a soft. It is as though a stereotyped Judge and a stereotyped Social Worker confront each other every time that responsibility is in question.

JUDGE: Mrs A stole two jewelled watches. Clearly didn't need to: she's well off. She could quite well have bought them.

There's no excuse for such people.

SOCIAL WORKER: Why would anyone do so irrational a thing if he could help it?

JUDGE: Nonsense. If she didn't want the watches, she wanted the excitement. Doing what you want is acting freely.

SOCIAL WORKER: She says she didn't want the excitement; she says she doesn't know what came over her. And she can't have wanted the excitement of getting caught: she's shattered, it's ruining her life.

JUDGE: She should have thought of that before. It was obvious enough.

SOCIAL WORKER: She's menopausal, you know . . .

JUDGE: So are thousands who don't steal.

SOCIAL WORKER: And some who do — and people differ . . .

JUDGE: Until we know more, we must treat everybody alike.

SOCIAL WORKER: Until we know more, we should give people who act irrationally the benefit of the doubt.

JUDGE: And let all the rational villains plead irrationality? — which is probably just what your Mrs A is doing anyway. . . . And that line won't get *B* off: he's a professional. Caught stripping lead from the Town Hall roof — he makes a good deal out of that kind of thing. Criminal type, record as long as your arm.

SOCIAL WORKER: Criminal background. Never had a chance.

JUDGE: Going by his record, he's had a good many.

SOCIAL WORKER: They can't have been real chances. Who would have B's values if he hadn't been brought up to them? And what about D? Penniless alcoholic: stole a bottle of whisky when he was desperate, poor man.

JUDGE: Whose fault is it that he was desperate? He ought to get a grip on himself.

SOCIAL WORKER: It may have been his fault once, but he can't help himself now.

JUDGE: Defeatism. Some people manage it; and if we all took *your* line no one would ever try.

And so on. Traditionally the (as it were) Judge has not often let us plead lack of freedom. Even when someone seems to be dramatically out of control there are ways of denying, if not the plea, then the lenience that *prima facie* should follow: possible fakers must be discouraged. One way is to see the trouble as something alien, which we must punish in order to drive it from its host. We do not blame *him* individually perhaps, but (just as if he were faking) he needs burning or beating — to free him from a devil or original sin, or madness taken as the sign of one or the other:

> On ye lordlie loftes of Bedlam
> with stubble softe & dainty,
> braue braceletts strong, sweet whips ding dong
> and wholesome hunger plenty . . .[100]

The ghost of this idea haunts John Doe and Joe Bloggs in my story: whether Doe is telling the truth or lying, there seem to be reasons why he should not be let off scot-free.

Only one plea stands a good chance with the Judge, because it does not appeal to that unverifiable thing, psychological compulsion. It is ignorance, acting in good faith. So for example among real Judges, when English law at last took madness for an extenuating condition, only delusion counted: see the House of Lords' McNaughton Rules 'incorporating . . . the famous dictum that if an offender knew that what he was doing was wrong then he was legally sane and subject to punishment'.[101] And although ignorance can extenuate in theory, the Judge may still be suspicious wherever it might be faked. It could always in theory be faked when it is said to be due to failure of mind rather than lack of data — like John Doe's sudden loss of memory.

The (as it were) Social Worker may plead that we have evidence enough to *know* that people sometimes cannot help themselves, even when they have the fullest data. The 1959 Mental Health Act in England is to some extent a victory of Social Worker over Judge, where madness is concerned, though perhaps not a great one.

With the abolition of the death penalty for murder, the question of whether an offender is mad or not may seem to some disinterested observers a somewhat academic question. . . . After all, to be pronounced sane and guilty merits a finite sentence in an orthodox prison with the possibility of parole. Not guilty by reason of insanity may result in a sentence of unknown length in an institution, designated a 'special hospital' but resembling in every other way an orthodox prison.[102]

(JUDGE: If you will guarantee that 'therapy' is at least as unpleasant as punishment, to discourage fakers, I'll oppose you a good deal less.

SOCIAL WORKER: I'm afraid I often can guarantee it.)

But the Social Worker has interest vested in Socrates. If, as Socrates claims, a man never does wrong except through ignorance, perhaps we can help him without unduly humiliating or hurting him, and at no impossible expense. So from Socrates onward we find bad or foolish behaviour explained (by some) as entirely due to things that better education might cure: an untrained rational soul which does not rule the passions as it could, an unruly Id which we may disarm by becoming conscious of it, 'false consciousness', a lack of 'insight' which teachers or (real) social workers might supply. . . . We have called Socrates' thesis a paradox since it first appeared, and still (it seems) we go on hoping.

We are therefore ambivalent about self-deceivers, at two levels. If the Judge and Social Worker points of view can agree on what counts as an extenuating condition, they may still fight wherever that condition might be faked; and they may also fight about what conditions are to count. Sartre — all Judge and no Social Worker — sets one limit: no excuses to be allowed except ignorance acting in good faith, and 'good faith' very narrowly defined. A determinist could (though not all determinists do) set the other: all Social Worker and no Judge, he could say that since nothing can ever be helped, the question of excuse does not arise at all. Most of us in theory, and I suspect nearly everyone in practice, are in a position to be torn; and so we may not know how to react even when we are nearly sure that the man who acts in the teeth of the evidence knows — knows freely — what he is doing. Must we then suppose that he can help himself? And if not always, when?

'Self-deception' may therefore feel like a label to solve many problems. Its suggestion that the man's contrary behaviour is due to ignorance, to being deceived, will quiet the Judge somewhat, and will give Socratic hope to the Social Worker. The claim that such ignorance is self-induced will at least pretend to explain its (often very obvious) look of means to an end. And once we call a man a self-deceiver we can stress whichever point of view — Social Worker or Judge — suits us at the time. He is an agent, or a victim. He is an ingenious deceiver, or he is strangely deceived. He is sincere but muddled, or he is worse than an ordinary liar: at least the liar is honest with himself. We can do all this only because 'self-deception' is contradictory, and so never more than a metaphor; but it may be a metaphor that we need.[103]

If so, we should nevertheless recognize that it is one: not a real description, but a license to improvise. The sensitive and adroit may improvise well by instinct; the thick-skinned, the clumsy, the self-righteous and so on can use the label's ambivalence to make wrong moves and feel justified. Moreover those implicit messages which soothe the Judge in us, and give hope to the Social Worker, are wishful thinking: on the evidence it seems clear that virtue is not knowledge, and knowledge does not necessarily make us responsible.[104]

We must be very careful. Knowledge — free knowledge — is at any rate *necessary* for virtue, for choosing what best fits reality, whatever 'best' means — or else virtue is an illusion, mere luck: we happen to hit a target we did not see. Free knowledge is necessary too for free choice, and free choice — whatever that may be — for responsibility. Now virtue may indeed be only luck. It must have an irreducible element of luck in any case, since, by the traditional sceptical arguments,[105] knowledge in the sense of *absolute* certainty is not attainable. But more radically, free choice (and so responsibility too) may be a chimera. I suspect that it is, but I do not see how we could prove it; nor do I see how we could ever act on that assumption. (See Appendix B.) This gives us a *prima facie* case against self-deception when it buries knowledge, or again when it compels us to act against what we know: in either case the agent can do the right thing *only* by luck, if at all, while at other times he may perhaps have a choice.

But when he seems to be in either state, he may be only pretending; and that pretence may sometimes be the best that he can do with his material, including not just himself and his own fate, probably, but other people and some part of theirs. Then again what if he does the right thing by luck, but his luck is his self-deception? Perhaps he has buried knowledge which he can cope with in no other way, or could not cope with so well — perhaps no one could otherwise cope with it so well; or he is compelled to do what he thinks is best when he might not, if he could help it. He may then prefer to have no choice, or later be glad that he had none. Think for example of someone whom pride compels to go on as though he will succeed, when he knows he may very well fail; or someone who goes on with confidence, because he has buried that same knowledge. He may after all have no choice in any case: freedom — or maybe freedom for him at this time — could be an illusion. If so, it is a question of which determinant is best; and it could be one of these.

Even when we are sure that somebody's self-deception is a bad thing, making him foolish or perverse, there may sometimes be no good way to stop him. Anyone who tells him the truth to his face must thereby admit knowing it himself, which at once rules out certain pretences: the only good ways to act may be among them. He will also be the speaker of bad news, the cause and witness of a loss of face. A self-deceiver is almost bound to take such things ungratefully: they are what he has been resisting. Perhaps no one who could tell him the truth can afford this, and there is no other way to let him know.

Again, thought, feeling, and action are rated differently by different people. So far I have considered only the *usefulness for action* of knowledge, for example; but we may have come to value such things for themselves, just as we value freedom from pain for itself, even against its natural function. (We might — the whole species might — some time prefer death to too much pain.) People's tactics and strategies in self-deception may vary widely because of such differences; and so may the ways in which we judge and treat them. Dr S for example is an entirely different self-deceiver from Mary McCarthy's Margaret Sargent, although in a way they have the same problem: scruples that condemn what they feel compelled to do.

That was what [her husband] had sent her to the doctor for — a perfectly simple little operation . . . to cut out the festering conscience, which was of no use to you at all and was only making you suffer . . . . All at once, she remembered that she had not told [the doctor] the end of her dream.

. . . There were three tall young men, all of them a sort of dun colour, awkward, heavy-featured, without charm, a little like the pictures of Nazi prisoners that the Soviet censor passes . . . .. One of the men came towards her, and she got up at once, her manner becoming more animated. In a moment she was flirting with him and telling one of the other girls 'Really he is not so bad as the others. He is quite interesting when you begin to talk to him'. His face changed . . . there was something Byronic about him. He bent down to kiss her; it was a coarse, loutish kiss . . . 'Perhaps I kissed the wrong one' and she looked up to find that . . . he was exactly like the others. But in a minute it happened again; his skin whitened, his thick, flat nose refined itself. . . . When he kissed her this time she kept her eyes shut, knowing very well what she would see if she opened them . . .

The memory of the dream struck her, like a heavy breaker. . . . 'Oh my God . . . how could I, how could I?' . . . She could not disown the dream. It belonged to her. If she had not yet embraced a captive Nazi, it was only an accident of time and geography, a lucky break. . . . And yet, she thought . . . she could still detect her own frauds. At the end of the dream, her eyes were closed, but the inner eye remained alert. She could still distinguish the Nazi prisoner from the English milord, even in the darkness of need.

'Oh, my God' she said . . . 'do not let them take this away from me. If the flesh must be blind, let the spirit see. Preserve me in disunity. *O di*' she said aloud, *reddite me hoc pro pietate mea*'.[106]

Where belief is mere acting and feeling, she will believe in the teeth of the evidence, because she must; but although it gives her pain, she wants to know it. Nor does she really want unity of spirit and flesh on the spirit's terms, if she could have it: the book as a whole makes it clear that she wants both sides. If (in an imperfect world) this means disunity, all that she asks is the strength to bear it.

Any moral or practical line that we take with self-deceivers must take account of these contingencies and innumerable others. I have never found one that does. Fingarette's fits a good many, and it may often be the most politic even where it does not: a Social Worker's theory — treat the self-deceiver as a victim, not an agent. In trying to stave off disintegration as a person, that is, as a moral agent, he has disavowed certain engagements in the world which he will not give up; in doing so, he has lost the power of free choice, and so the moral agency that he was trying to save. He needs professional help.

The medical aim is . . . in substance a spiritual aim. It is to help the individual become an agent and cease being a patient. . . . Insofar as [the moralists] presume the self-deceiver to be fully a personal agent in the matter at hand, they preach, teach and argue in vain. . . .

What the self-deceiver lacks is not concern nor integrity but some combination of courage and a way of seeing how to approach his dilemma without probable disaster to himself. . . . [He] must be helped to go to the limits of his courage, but not provoked beyond the breaking point.[107]

But this assumes that both in theory and in practice he *can* be made free; that if freedom exists, we can see when it is absent; that when he is made free — or cannot pretend any more that he is not — he and those whom his self-deception affects must be better off; and that morality's first aim — its *sine qua non*, which it may try deceiving itself to protect — is the integration (in the person) of all avowed engagements in the world. It seems to require a simpler world, and people more alike than they are.

As for freedom, I think that we do not know it exists; and if it does, we do not know when and where. We can speak with confidence only about particular freedoms from specific constraints. And if the constraints are psychological, once again we do not know whether they bind absolutely or not. Nor do we often know whether they bind for good or ill, though 'common sense' has certain rules of thumb. As well as a *prima facie* case for free knowledge, we have one against acts which seem to clash with the agent's usual tastes, standards, beliefs, or with those we think 'normal', if we do not know his in particular. If some of him would rather not do what he does, we know at least that he is not entirely happy; we also know that such inconsistency often brings trouble to other people. But I think that we cannot presume much more: the world is imperfect and mysterious, self-deceivers are very various and, beyond a certain point, inscrutable. For the same reason that we have chosen a paradox to name them, we have no obvious way to judge them. I suspect (to borrow a phrase from T.S. Eliot on aesthetics[108]) that 'there is no method, except to be very intelligent'.

APPENDIX A

(1) SOURCES FOR CASE HISTORIES (MULTIPLE PERSONALITY)
(2) THE 'SPLIT BRAIN' MODEL FOR SELF-DECEPTION

(1) *Multiple personality*

The most useful general survey that I have found is an article by W.S. Taylor and M.F. Martin.[109] They define the condition roughly as that of an individual with 'two or more personalities each of which is so well developed and integrated as to have a relatively co-ordinated, rich, unified and stable life of its own', and continue:

Until psychological methods develop sufficiently to make a more precise definition possible, perhaps no two students in combing the literature would draw up identical lists of cases. Our rough definition, however, excludes many cases which seem too simply hypnotic, narrowly hysterical, evidently organic or psychotic, likely faked, or insufficiently described to be called multiple personality.[110]

From 'the literature most available to American psychologists' they arrive at a list of 76 cases, adding that a sampling of the *Index Medicus* suggests that the medical journals of the world contain at least as many more. There have also been a number of cases recorded since their article was published. From all this it seems that multiple personality is a rare condition, but not too rare to have produced a respectable set of independent reports. Taylor and Martin comment:

The subjects [known to the authors], including those not listed here, number more than a hundred. These . . . are widely distributed in time and space. Most of them had never heard of other cases. A number of the subjects are uncommonly high-minded, honest people (e.g. Cases 12, 19, 30, 47 and 68). Likewise, the observers number more than a hundred; they, too, are widely distributed; many of them know little or nothing of one another's work; and most of them have been accustomed to watching for fraud and to maintaining professional standards. Finally, many of the cases have been judged independently by different observers; and among all the various cases, there are essential parallels in the records for each type of multiple personality.[111]

Case 47 is Mary Reynolds; 68 is Thomas Hanna. The parallels in the records allow a system of classification, which they introduce as follows:

Symbols	*Meanings*
A	Alternating personality
C	Coconscious personality
I	Intraconscious personality
M	Mutually amnesic
O	One-way amnesic
P	Propriety (good behaviour)
Q	Quality of personality (temperament, sociability, values, etc.)
R	Responses (automatic acts, paralyses, etc.)
S	Sensibility (paresthesias, anasthesias etc.)
X	'Sex' (one personality professedly masculine, another feminine; or one heterosexual, another homosexual, etc.)
Y	Youthfulness (one personality seeming more youthful or childlike than another).

Thus, if the fabled case of Dr Jekyll and Mr Hyde appeared in the list as:
  '77 R.L. Stevenson   Dr Jekyll and Mr Hyde 2 A M QP'
it would mean that the case numbered 77, recounted by Robert Louis Stevenson and called Dr Jekyll and Mr Hyde, had two personalities which alternated with each other, were mutually amnesic, showed differences in general quality and propriety.[112]

A seventh column refers to discussions in the bibliography: over a hundred references to books and papers in academic journals.

One such book is William McDougall's *Outline of Abnormal Psychology*.[113] I have quoted several of his summaries (longer than those in Taylor and Martin) of the older cases. He considers multiple personality to be of great theoretical importance, and therefore gives it more space than do most writers on abnormal psychology. His general theory of consciousness and dissociation seems to be a Philonous one,[114] but he keeps case histories separate from his interpretation of them; his interest only ensures that they are given in detail, with many quotes from original sources and some from their critics. These remarks about Miss Beauchamp are typical.

I would emphasize the point that I accept Dr Prince's descriptions, although in regard to his interpretations I venture to differ in certain respects. It has been suggested by many critics that, in the course of Dr Prince's long and intimate dealing with the case, involving as it did the frequent use of hypnosis, both for exploratory and therapeutic processes, he may have moulded the course of its development to a degree that cannot be determined. This possibility cannot be denied.[115]

Perhaps it cannot be denied of any long involvement of this kind, where the observer is also a therapist. Prince's study of Miss Beauchamp[116] is in any case by far the most detailed history that is available. If I have usually preferred Eve Black to Sally Beauchamp as an example of co-consciousness (etc.), it is because the case of 'Evelyn Lancaster' has also been reported in detail, by the patient as well as her therapist; also I wanted one fairly recent report.

The original account by Drs. Thigpen and Cleckley, in the *Journal of Abnormal and Social Psychology* for 1954, is fleshed out in their book *The Three Faces of Eve* in a popular style which does not always inspire confidence. Moreover 'Eve' herself, whose real name is Christine Costner Sizemore, published her own autobiography in 1977, and at times it varies widely from *The Three Faces of Eve*. If we are to believe the patient herself, the background of *Three Faces* is often dangerously inaccurate 'to hide her identity, [but] that was wrong; the truth should be told just exactly as it happened, not distorted'.[117] The case seems to have been a good deal more complex than it is made to appear, and the alleged 'cure' at its end was really nothing of the kind: it took many years more and a different therapist.

. . . The book indicates that the three personalities were all that ever existed. That's all wrong; there were nine whom I can remember before them; and Chris Black, Chris White and Jane make twelve! The doctors think that there were always just the two Chrises and then Jane came; and that when they died Jane became the last one. . . . But the biggest mistake of all was about her being well [at the end of the book]. She was not well at all, nothing had changed except that the new personality who came was an entirely different one from all the others: No. 13! . . . There were still voices, headaches, suicide attempts; and even Dr Thigpen did not understand that. . . . Why did he keep telling her that she was well?[118]

(Dr Thigpen's attitude to his patient, after he had recorded her 'cure' in a best-seller, seems from the patient's own account as choice a case of self-deception as any in this book.) An alleged sequel by 'Eve' herself, *The Final Face of Eve*, [119] was apparently edited without the author's knowledge to match the first book, and is dismissed in her autobiography as worthless.

When Chris received her first copy of the book, it was the first time she had seen the edited material. After Dr Thigpen had made his corrections, he had sent the copy on to Jim [James Poling, a professional writer who collaborated with Chris herself], so Chris was aware of no corrections other than her own. This book was as much of a disappointment to her as had been the first book — it was, in fact, essentially the same book, bearing none of the changes or corrections that had been the impetus behind its inception. . . . The ending was a lie.[120]

I have used only material about which Dr Thigpen and Chris Costner Sizemore agree.

(2) *The 'Split Brain' model for self-deception*

At the end of *Self-Deception*, Fingarette seems to have reached a Philonous position, I think without adequate evidence. The Appendix to his book may help explain why he finds this plausible, although he says that he reached his philosophical conclusions independently. It is called 'The Neuropsychological Context of Self-Deception', and it links his theory of spelling-out with certain now famous experiments by Sperry, Gazzaniga and others.[121] The subjects were epileptic patients, whose brain hemispheres had been separated by cutting the *corpus callosum*. His discussion is necessarily limited to his special interest and is in any case tentative, since research in this field is only beginning. He gives a bibliography for interested readers, to which I think we should now add Stuart Dimond's *The Double Brain* (a synthesis of at least a good deal — for all I know, all — the major research in the field up to 1972, with a very much larger bibliography) and a philosophical discussion: Thomas Nagel's 'Brain Bisection and the Unity of Consciousness'.[122]

To sum up even more briefly than Fingarette does: the right and left hemispheres of the brain can function separately, and they work to some extent in parallel. The left half (very roughly) controls the right side of the body and *vice versa*. Both hemispheres also seem able to handle concepts and language in some ways; but only one — generally the left — seems to govern active speech and 'the more intellectually elaborate performances of human beings'.[123] (In the cases to which Fingarette refers, the left hemisphere seems always to have been dominant.) When the hemispheres are physically cut off from each other, information given to one hand, one half of the visual field, and so on, seems to register only with the hemisphere that rules it: for only those parts of the body which that hemisphere also rules will react appropriately. And if it is not the 'speech' hemisphere, the individual cannot *say* what he has seen or touched; but he may still show recognition in other ways. These may involve language, though not active speech. For example 'the examiner would read (aloud) "Used to tell time", and would then flash five choice words in succession to the left visual field. In this instance the patients [although they could not speak the word] made a correct manual signal to the word "clock".'[124] Two more things are important.

[1] Not only can the person [*sic*] understand language and respond skilfully, but he will show appropriate emotion. Thus, during a sequence of photos flashed to the left visual field, the subject blushes and smiles with embarrassment when unexpectedly a photo of a nude woman is presented. But in response to questions, the subject says she does not know why she is smiling, and didn't see anything. (This may be observed in a film prepared by Professor Gazzaniga.)[125]

[2] The experiments are replete with instances in which the left hemisphere, deprived of direct information, proposes ingenious guesses or rationalizations which can be demonstrated to be dependent on specific, indirect clues, or to be quite unreliable.[126]

For example, in the experiment just quoted, a patient whose left hand had correctly signalled 'clock' was asked to say what word he had seen. His left hemisphere had seen nothing, but had heard the clue 'used to tell time'; he said 'watch'.

Fingarette thinks that these results suggest that spelling-out is 'a relatively autonomous skill' compared to other uses of language like reading, and that it is more specifically located in the brain.

Further, we need to assume that a similar functional divorce between an individual's engagement and his linguistic expression of that engagement need not require *physical* cutting of intra-cerebral communication but could be 'psychogenic'. The behavioural evidence concerning self-deception, and defense and the unconscious, strongly suggest that such communication can in fact be damped down, distorted, or cut off by 'psychological' means . . .

As research workers in the field have noted, one inevitably begins [when the hemispheres are separated and experiments of the Gazzaniga kind are done] to talk . . . as if each were a separate individual. This . . . is supported by a number of related experiments, e.g. the non-transferable learning which can go in one hemisphere independently of, but concurrently with a different learning sequence going on in the other. In all this, the parallelism to our talk about the division of the psyche in defence and in self-deception is notable.

More generally, it should be noted that the left hemisphere is associated with the more intellectually elaborate performances of human beings. Calculation, and abstract reasoning of a high order, seems generally to be rooted in left-hemisphere functions. Finally . . . the left hemisphere seems to be dominant with respect to the co-ordination of projects which are themselves defined in complex and abstract intellectual terms rather than in fairly specific motor terms. All of this generally coincides with the thesis that spelling-out is, more than other forms of language and concept use, intimately associated with the self, the highest-order organization and unity of the individual human being.[127]

(This shows why I find 'person' odd in quote [1]: there the *right* hemisphere is the one whose responses Fingarette describes.)

Besides this parallel between disavowal and severed hemispheres, he suggests one between a patient who has had a pre-frontal lobotomy and the sociopath — the opposite in a way to a self-deceiver — who spells out but does not feel concern about his engagements. This second point is made so briefly that I only mention it, as a thing which certainly seems to warrant study; it is the first that I want to discuss.

If the 'deceiver' (A₁) is really like that part of the patient which pointed to 'clock' or smiled at a nude picture, we might well decide that it or he was independently conscious: on the face of it, this is conscious behaviour. But only on the face of it: I think it is too simple to be conclusive, if this is all the evidence that we have. If the patient was able to convince observers that this hemisphere was conscious, I think it must have been because his — or its — behaviour was part of a more complex sequence.

But in any case we canot simply equate dissociation (of all kinds relevant to self-deception) with a functional split between the hemispheres, whose symptoms is some loss or avoidance of active speech. Multiple personality shows this. Of course alternating personalities like Mary Reynolds cannot both speak at once; but each speaks as well as the other. If we wanted to imagine her condition paralleled by some division of the brain, it would have to be not a simple split of right *versus* left, but one with a fluctuating border, so that each included the 'speech centre' in turn. But even this seems far-fetched: so far as we know, *all* behaviour was controlled by each personality in turn. So, on the face of it, each had access to all the main features of the brain. Again, a right-left split cannot explain Eve Black 'speaking' to Eve White, when Eve White herself was awake and articulate. (It will not explain a schizophrenic's auditory hallucinations either, when they are not memories and when the 'hearer' is also able to talk, and when what the 'voices' say makes sense; for I suppose that 'active speech' must mean any intelligent framing of thoughts in words, not simply mouth-talk.) If we went on to suggest that in cases like Eve's there might (abnormally) be a 'speech centre' in each hemisphere, we would still have trouble with triplet and quadruplet personalities.

On the other hand, some of the cases reported by Taylor and Martin seem to confirm that multiple personality may in some ways divide up the brain.

Differences [of sensibility] appear in so many cases, and occur so consistently in other forms of dissociation, that we wonder whether these differences have not merely been overlooked in the few cases for which they are not reported.

Mrs. X (Case 75), when about to give birth to a child without anaesthetic, slipped into her 'Susie' personality because Susie never felt pain. Sally Beauchamp . . . felt no fatigue. She was also analgesic and tactually anaesthetic except when either visual or auditory stimuli accompanied the stimuli for pain and touch. Blanche Witman (Case 33) in one phase was analgesic, totally anaesthetic, without muscle sense, deaf in one ear, weak-visioned in one eye, wholly colour blind, and so on.

Differences in . . . responses considered particularly, are no less common. . . . Blanche Witman . . . in one personality was paralyzed, and in the other, normal. . . . In many a case of multiple personality, at least one of the personalities does automatic writing. . . . One case (Case 7) in one phase was ambidextrous and understood English only, but in the other phase was left-handed and spoke Welsh.[128]

Some of these differences — handedness, language, automatic writing — also suggest a division related to the separate hemispheres. But even if this were so, it often seems not a case of right *versus* left but of some other pattern. The ambidextrous personality, for example, would presumably have well-developed hand control in both hemispheres, his left-handed partner in one; but it was the left-handed personality who was bilingual. This rules out the possibility of a speech centre in each half (which would be most abnormal, but then so is multiple personality). Since we are told that he was left-handed, not that he had the use only of his left hand, we must suppose that he had normal minor-hand control of the right hand as well. — And so on.

Anyway I have argued that self-deception (like multiple personality, and unlike a split brain) need not cripple our speech at all. Disavowal seems to take many forms, of many degrees of articulacy; and — *pace* Fingarette — it can include spelling-out. If the words which we use to spell-out can be 'cryptic or allusive' it may indeed *often* include spelling-out. And spelling-out does not always use words, so perhaps we should not associate it as closely as Fingarette does with that one part of the brain. This may be so even if its 'model' is active speech; for other parts of the brain may rule things which are like speech in the relevant ways. Violin fingering — Fingarette's own example of something we can spell out without words — is done by the left hand and so (we may suppose) ruled by the right hemisphere. It might be possible to test whether a split-brain patient can spell it out, for example by concentrating in the way that it takes to learn something new.

Finally, Fingarette rather simplifies the picture when he places speech unequivocally in the left hemisphere. Besides cases where it turns up in the right instead, there is evidence that in children — possibly up to nine or ten years old — the hemispheres have equal potential, and in some ways equal actual use.[129] Fingarette's simplification may not affect his thesis, but I am not sure. For example, if disavowal is (as he says) a return to the child's way with engagements, might it not involve some return to a less centralized command of spelling-out? This would fit my picture of self-deception better than his.

I agree that *some* ways of not spelling-out are strikingly like the ways of patients in 'split brain' experiments. Both in turn are also like artificial splits made by hypnosis — for example the behaviour of B before he opens the window.[130] This backs up the suggestion that a surgical cut-off may be copied 'psycho-genically'; as research in such things goes on, no doubt we shall learn more. But given the range of behaviour and thought that 'self-deception' covers, I do not think that it will ever show quite the hemisphere-correlation that Fingarette suggests.

APPENDIX B (1) 'VIRTUE IS KNOWLEDGE'
(2) 'IF YOU KNEW, YOU WERE RESPONSIBLE'

(1) *'Virtue is Knowledge'* (the Socratic 'paradox' and Social Worker's hope).
Virtue must be free knowledge if any, because the pivot is belief.

[SOCRATES] No one who either knows or believes that other things (which are in his power) are better than those he is doing, goes on doing them . . . [And]no one from choice [*hekōn*] goes after bad things, or things that he thinks are bad; it seems to me not in human nature to prefer [*ethelein*] to go after what one thinks bad rather than what one thinks good. And when one has to choose between two evils, no one will take the greater when he can take the less.[131]

'Good' here is defined as 'beneficial to the agent' and this in turn is taken to mean 'leading to a painless and pleasant life'.[132] This makes altruism seem a counterexample, on the face of it; but I think we can get round that. For a start we can go at least some way with Thomas Love Peacock's Mr Mac Laurel:

MR ESCOT: I believe it is generally admitted that one of the ingredients of justice is disinteredness.
MR MAC LAUREL: It is na admetted, sir, amang the pheelosophers of Edinbroo', that there is ony sic thing as desenteredness in the warld, or that a mon can care for onything sae much as his ain sel . . . Twa men, sir, shall purchase a piece o' grund atween 'em, and ae mon shall cover his half wi' a park . . . an' shall keep it a' for his ain sel: an' the other mon shall divide his half into leetle farms —
MR ESCOT: . . . and build a cottage on each of them, and cover his land with a simple, innocent and smiling population, who shall owe, not only their happiness, but their very existence, to his benevolence —
MR MAC LAUREL: Exactly, sir; an' ye will ca' the first mon selfish, an' the second desenterested; but the pheelosophical truth is semply this, that the ane is pleased wi' looking at trees, an' the other wi' seeing people happy an' comfortable.[133]

— especially if we remember that not only do tastes differ, and degrees of sensitivity to other people's feelings, but moral ideas too (Mr Mac Laurel calls this a man's 'ain notions o' the moral an' poleetical fetness o' things'[134]); also that guilt, shame and embarassment are forms of distress, while self-approval and the approval of others are typically pleasant. If this still does not seem to cover everything, we may go on to allow that what people think good may not be so simply linked to Plato's 'painless and pleasant life'; we can still take 'good', 'best' and so forth in a way that keeps the main point. It is that *what we think best, we also think should be the case; and we think that if the choice is ours, that is what we should choose*. The real challenge to Socrates comes I think not from Mr Mac Laurel's philanthropist or Florence Nightingale, but from all the people like me who deny, from experience, that it is 'not in human nature' to choose sometimes the thing we believe is worse. '*Video meliora proboque*', says Ovid's Medea, '*Deteriora sequor*'.[135] And the only easy 'Socratic' answer begs the question: 'But you can't *really* know (believe, understand) that X is better, because you chose Y!'

Given human contrariness, human perversity, why should we listen to Socrates at all? (And I think that few who follow him do so without a qualm.) Why have we called his alleged law of human nature a *paradox* ('contrary to appearances') and not just false? Compare that chief of Greek paradoxists, Zeno: in every case he professes to show by strict logic that a thing we often see — or think we do — cannot happen.[136] We see fast runners overtake slow ones for example; but give a tortoise a start on Achilles, and when Achilles reaches the tortoise's starting point (T_1) the tortoise will have crawled to a farther point (T_2); when Achilles gets to T_2 the tortoise will have gone on (a shorter way, but still gone on) to T_3, *ad infinitum*. The space between them grows smaller and smaller, but how — by this plausible account— can it ever reach zero and Achilles catch the tortoise?[137] What parallel logical or pseudo-logical case have Socratics against the likes of Medea?

There is the question-begging use of '*really* know' (or 'understand' or 'believe') that I gave above, though this may be less a persuader to the Socratic position than a sign that one holds it already. Apart from that, we have (most of us) the Social

Worker's hope; and we have equivocal modal terms in most (I suspect in all) European languages, starting with ancient Greek — other languages too perhaps, but the paradox is traditionally European. With their help it is not hard to confuse logical and empirical necessity, and I think that this is at the root of it.

Suppose that I know or believe that X is the right thing to do on occasion Y; — 'right' in any usual sense, including Plato's. A logical relation is involved (unless the claim is that I believe or 'know' without reason: not the thing at issue here). It connects my code of values — of what is 'right' in the given sense — and the ways that I would describe X and Y to myself. A code is general, and so are the descriptions insofar as they relate to it: if X is the right thing to do in Y, it must be because, given my values, this *sort* or thing is right for that sort of occasion. Such general relations are placeless and timeless, like $2 + 2 = 4$: a different logic may be involved, but not different in that way. They hold — or if they are more like $2 + 2 = 10$, are of a type to hold but fail to — between such things as concepts or terms, abstract from any given piece of thinking or saying. (A Platonist might say instead that they hold between Forms; but Forms are placeless and timeless too.) If the relation in question is a true one then, it will be so always, whether I come to exist or not and whether or not Y ever arises. If Y does arise, it will be true irrespective of what I actually do. On the other hand *my coming to know or believe* that Y *is* this sort of occasion, *my applying my code* and *concluding* that X is the right thing to do, and (whatever I do) my *acting*, are all particular events in time; at least some aspects of them also in space. Laws of physics apply to them. The relations between them may be causal or something less determining, but they cannot be logical: that is another category. And there is no reason *a priori* why the relation between events must reflect that other, placeless and timeless, logical relation, even if I have the logical relation in mind when the events take place. That is to say, there is no reason *a priori* why we should expect me always to do what I logically know to be right.

Only an argument from design or quasi-design can bridge this kind of gap. For example '$2 + 2 = 4$' states a logical relation; by contrast the relation between someone's pressing *these* keys on a calculator and getting *that* shape of green light in its window is causal, a question of mechanics. If we know the logical relation we can predict the causal one, but only because we know that the machine was built to express such relations. If its designer had wanted to misrepresent them instead, or to express something else — an aesthetic relation perhaps, based on the shapes of numerals — he could as well have made his machine flash '22' (say) when we pressed the '2 + 2' keys. Machines may also lose or lack definite programming, and there again we would not expect the logical answer when we press the keys. But we have no parallel argument from design that can save the Socratic paradox.

Plato's Socrates and perhaps the real one[138] did believe that nature must be explained in terms of a designer, with some kind of objective 'best' as his model.

I once heard someone reading from a book . . . by Anaxagoras, and asserting that it is mind that produces order and is the cause of everything. This explanation pleased me. Somehow it seemed right that mind should be the cause of everything, and I reflected that if this is so, mind in producing order . . . arranges each individual thing in the way that is best for it. Therefore if anyone wished to discover the reason why any given thing came or ceased or continued to be, he must find out how it was best for that thing to be. . . .[139]

Plato in the *Timaeus* calls this mind the Demiurge or 'craftsman', though he takes care to say that such terms are not literal truth, but likely analogues for what cannot be more exactly said.[140] And we might expect such a craftsman to shape human nature like the rest, so far as he could: 'for the best', that is — *ex hypothesi* — Socratically. But this only kicks the paradox upstairs. Not only do we need a valid argument for any shaping mind at all, and notoriously there is none; if we start from that hypothesis, we need one that will show why this mind in turn might not sometimes choose the worse and not the better, most particularly when designing us. Plato says only that the Demiurge was good, and the good are without jealousy: '. . . and being free from jealousy, he desired that all things should be as like himself as could be'.[141] If we ask in turn why *that* should be true, we never get more (I think) from Plato than some form of what Socrates says in the *Phaedo* passage: 'Somehow it seemed right'; and this so thoroughly begs the question that I suspect it is not meant as an argument. I think in fact that Plato did not base his Socratic thesis on the Demiurge, but *vice versa*.

Any theory which (like Plato's) allows the shaping or creating mind to be somehow less than perfect will have this flaw: we could be its choice for the worse, or its failure, or its mistake. Any that by contrast insists that it is perfect (like the Christian tradition) can only explain contrary human beings by trying to put the blame on *them*. And if this can be done at all, it must deny Socrates' 'law': they must sometimes knowingly choose the worse when they can choose the better or it is God's fault, not theirs.

Finally the Socratics need an argument to show that rational behaviour *is* what their designer — whoever or whatever that is — takes for its 'best'. This may sabotage them all; it certainly sabotages those I have not discussed so far, whose Demiurge is only somehow *like* a mind: evolution for example. A mindless 'designer's' 'goals' may be inferred only from what it in fact produces, and how. Our evolution's 'good' for example is presumably our species' survival — *a priori*, no more than that; which gives us no reason *a priori* why we must have evolved Socratically. (Given the dangerous things that humans seem able to value and to believe, that may indeed put it too lightly.) If we want to know whether or not evolution has shaped us that way, we can only go by what in fact we do — and so back to Medea.

To believe the Socratic paradox then, or even to call it a paradox, is I think to see things teleologically in a way that we should not, on the evidence. I have said that terms equivocal between logic and the empirical may help to confuse us in this; but when the logic is also being used to tell us what is *best*, such equivocation serves a wider, more familiar confusion between how things are and how we would like them to be. And once again words, in all the languages I know, help this confusion. Consider for instance the ambiguity in English of phrases like 'At her age she *should* be interested in boys'; There *must* be a Reason for it all!'; and 'You *can't* be sick here, sir!' (*'Can't I? Watch me!'*) In this context Plato's and Socrates' 'It seemed right to me' (*edoxe moi eu echein*) is completely at home.

To confuse what is with what should be is the formula for wishful thinking, if nothing more perverse. Given our tangled language (wishfully tangled, perhaps), I think that 'wishful thinking' is usually strong enough — especially when we note that *some* sort of teleology or quasi-teleology can be seen in nature, even if not the kind we hope; and that in fact we get safely through the day by *usually* doing what we think is right, in some sense of 'think' and a practical sense of 'right'. We cross the road when there is a gap between cars; we eat the toast, not the soap. . . . Even at this level, however, Socraticism is not inevitable: a fear of heights may keep someone from jumping out of the flames into the firemen's net though he *must* jump, to live. (According to Stanley Milgram, there are even people who cannot leave a burning house with their pants off.[142]) Sometimes we can explain such cases away, begging the question not too obviously: 'Jumping must have seemed worse to him than death by fire!'. If not, we may still (in hope) think of them as atypical, and then by an easy slide see them teleologically as human nature gone *wrong*, as a machine goes wrong. This is still wishful thinking: when we see the desirable as the normal, it seems easier to reach. (But if we could agree that people *should* behave Socratically, and learn enough about ourselves to become our own designers, we might make it come true.)

(2) *'If you knew, you were responsible'* (the Judge's Rule).

I think that the Socratic paradox makes sense (as opposed to being true) only as a form of psychological determinism. If we can choose freely at all, it must then be only between things that we value equally. The Judge by contrast wants to hold wrong-doers responsible, which must mean that they have broken the Socratic 'law' and chosen to do wrong when they did not have to — in other words freely. Attempts to define 'responsible' in a way that gets round this seem to me misconceived and doomed to fail: in so redefining the word, we lose the concept, just as we lose the concept 'freedom' if we try to redefine it so that it is compatible with determinism. To quote Isaiah Berlin:

. . . it seems patently inconsistent to assert, on the one hand, that all events are wholly determined to be what they are by other events . . . and, on the other, that men are free to choose between at least two courses of possible action — free not merely in the sense of being able to do what they choose to do (and because they choose to do it), but in the sense of not being determined to choose what they choose by causes outside their control. If it is held that every act of will or choice is fully determined by its respective antecedents . . . this belief is incompatible with the notion of choice held by ordinary men and by philosophers when they are not consciously defending a determinist position.

More particularly, I see no way round the fact that the habit of giving moral praise or blame . . . with the implication that [people] are responsible for [their acts], since they need not have acted as they did . . . would be undermined by belief in determinism.[143]

Now 'free' in the required sense is a word that I do not understand. If we define it simply as 'not determined', random events are free; but this has nothing to do with responsibility. The alternative is to abstract a concept of absolute freedom from our concepts of particular freedoms: from manacles, from the fear of heights that will not let me jump into the firemen's net, from the Secret Police who will shoot me and my family if I am seen escaping from that special burning house, from the fear for myself and my family (to put it another way) which combines with my knowledge of the Secret Police to keep me inside, from the delusion that I am a salamander, from the mistaken idea that my friends can get in to save me, or simply from the laws of physics, which we might expect to rule my body's movements, whatever they are. . . . But every particular freedom is compatible with determinism of a different kind — even the last, since psychological causes could still rule us, even if the laws of physics were mysteriously waived for human action. If we go on to abstract to 'freedom from *all* determining factors', however, 'free' acts again might really be only random — unless we define freedom *ad hoc* as 'the relation between events which is neither indeterminacy nor cause'; and that begs the question.

For why after all should there be any such relation? The imagination has no room for it. Think of trying to simulate it on a computer: what could we do but program either 'choices' that were caused, or random ones? And what sequence of human acts could we not in theory simulate by some combination of these? But if a machine can in theory act as we do without freedom, so can we. It is a possible account, and simpler, and less mysterious.

Nor do I see how it can help to say that we act for reasons instead of being caused, as we are caused (say) to sneeze when we breathe in pepper. This is only to say that the events which lead to action typically include the agent's somehow coming to take account of a logical relation and deciding to mirror it in what he does (see section (1) above). It says nothing about how this happens, but only that it does (or fails to); and how it happens is the point at issue. Nor does it help (*pace* Sartre) to derive the idea of freedom from that of consciousness: there is nothing in the idea of consciousness that suggests one might not take over a conscious being's body and run it like a machine, determining even his thoughts by determining his brain — while he stayed conscious.

We may feel that there *must* be a third possible relation between events, neither cause nor its mere absence, because (as Berlin says) responsibility demands it. So it does, and so responsibility may be an illusion: I am bound to say that I think it probably is. If so, knowledge obviously does not make people responsible for what they do.

Probability falls short of proof though; and given the phenomenal emptiness of the concept 'freedom', what could a proof that it did not exist be like? And perhaps we cannot survive without some assumption that people are responsible for what they do. 'Fatalism has not bred passivity in Moslems, nor has determinism sapped the vigour of Calvinists or Marxists, although some Marxists feared that it might. Practice sometimes belies profession, no matter how sincerely held.'[144] 'Common sense' so far as I know is never consistently determinist. Suppose we allow then that there may be such a thing as freedom: a mystery (as if cause and indeterminacy were not mysterious enough). This is wishful thinking, but conceivably we could be lucky: it could be true; and if we need it, we might as well act on that assumption. For suppose that we do: if we had any choice in so doing, the assumption is right; and if it is wrong, we were bound to do it anyway.

The Judge's Rule, however, goes well beyond that, and too far. It is wishful thinking again no doubt, for it is obviously attractive: if all that we need to be able to do right is knowledge, then knowledge will not save everyone perhaps; but it will save everyone who deserves it. But if knowledge does make us responsible, we must *always* be free to act on what we know; and if freedom is probably a chimera and at best a mystery, we cannot claim anything so definite. Even if freedom exists, when and where it exists is still in doubt. As always, all we have to go by is what people do and (with caution) what they feel; and these are — to put it most wishfully — inconclusive.

NOTES

1. Béla Szabados 'Wishful Thinking and Self-Deception' (*Analysis*, 1973), p. 201.
2. *Ibid.* p. 205.
3. Herbert Fingarette, *Self-Deception* (Routledge & Kegan Paul, London, 1969).
4 Raphael Demos 'On Lying to Oneself' (*The Journal of Philosophy*, September 1960), pp. 588ff.
5. *Ibid.* pp. 594–5.
6. Jean-Paul Sartre, *L'Etre et le néant* (NFR/Gallimard, Paris, 1943); English translation by Hazel E. Barnes, *Being and Nothingness* (Methuen, London, 1957), p. 49.
7. Sonnet CXXXVIII, *The Complete Works of William Shakespeare* (ed. W.S. Craig, Oxford University Press, London, 1952), p. 1125.
8. Rebecca West, *The Fountain Overflows* (Macmillan, London, 1958), p. 33.
9. Gilbert Ryle, *The Concept of Mind* (Hutchinson, London, 1949), pp. 133–5.
10. Alfred J. Ayer, *The Problem of Knowledge* (Macmillan, London, 1956), pp. 11–15, 31–2.
11. William McDougall, *Outline of Abnormal Psychology* (Methuen, London, 1926).
12. W.S. Taylor and M.F. Martin, 'Multiple Personality' (*The Journal of Abnormal and Social Psychology*, 1944), pp. 281–300.
13. *Ibid.* p. 283.
14. McDougall, *op. cit.* p. 484.
15. Bernard Williams, *Problems of the Self* (Cambridge University Press, London, 1973), pp. 15ff.
16. See for example the case of Thomas Hanna (McDougall *op. cit.* pp. 484–7, Taylor and Martin *op. cit.* pp. 287–8) and my Examples 2 and 3.
17. Morton Prince, *The Unconscious: the fundamentals of human personality normal and abnormal* (Macmillan, New York, 1921), pp. 545–663. See also McDougall, *op. cit.* pp. 491ff. and Taylor and Martin, *op. cit.* pp. 287–9.
18. McDougall, *op. cit.* pp. 492–3.
19. And other legal documents. See C.H. Thigpen and H. Cleckley, *The Three Faces of Eve* (Popular Library, New York, 1961), pp. 154ff.
20 C.H. Thigpen and H. Cleckley, 'A Case of Multiple Personality' (*The Journal of Abnormal and Social Psychology*, January 1954), pp. 135–151.
21. See note 19. The book was published more or less at the same time as the

release of a film based on it (Twentieth Century Fox).

22. Evelyn Lancaster (pseudonym) with James W. Poling, *The Final Face of Eve* (McGraw-Hill, New York, 1958); title in Britain *Strangers in My Body* (Secker & Warburg, London, 1958). The British title was the author's own choice.

23. Chris Costner Sizemore with Elen Sain Petillo, *I'm Eve* (Jove/Harcourt Brace Jovanovich, New York, 1978).

24. *The Three Faces of Eve*, p. 66.

25. Morton Prince, *The Dissociation of a Personality: a boigraphical study in abnormal psychology* (Longmans, New York, 1905), *passim*.

26. *Ibid.* pp. 162ff.; cf. *The Three Faces of Eve*, pp 88–9. Sally's power was also limited however: "'I make her do all sorts of things", she boasted. "I made her drink three glasses of wine last night, — she never drinks but one — and then I tried to make her talk and tell everything she knew . . . I could not make her do it, but I tried"' (*The Dissociation of a Personality*, p. 59).

27. 'A Case of Multiple Personality', pp. 142–3. On the 'voice', see also *The Three Faces of Eve*, p. 66 and *I'm Eve*, pp. 272 ff.

28. McDougall, *op. cit.* pp. 94–5. See also Fred H. Frankel: *Hypnosis: Trance as a Coping Mechanism* (Plenum, London & New York, 1976), pages in index *s.v.* 'multiple personality', 'post-hypnotic suggestion' etc.

29. *Ibid.* pp. 484ff.; Taylor and Martin, *op. cit.* pp. 287–8.

30. McDougall, *op. cit.* p. 484.

31. Taylor and Martin, *op. cit.* p. 289.

32. Miss Beauchamp's 'B₁' is a case in point: see McDougall, *op. cit.* pp. 497–8. For the second, see *The Three Faces of Eve*, pp. 186–7 and 193–4, and *I'm Eve* pp. 27ff. (Both these however tend to support Thigpen and Cleckley's view that 'no single incident of fright and stress, such as our patient's experience [when forced to touch her dead grandmother] can plausibly be assumed to account in full for the disorder. . . . As a working hypothesis let us consider it likely that many advance influences had already contributed to a serious conflict. . . .' (*The Three Faces of Eve*, pp. 195–6.)

33. Sigmund Freud, *The Psychopathology of Everyday Life* (The Standard Edition of the Complete Psychoanalytic Works of Sigmund Freud, eds. J. Strachey and A. Freud, Hogarth Press, London, *Vol. VI*, 1960).

34. Sigmund Freud, *The Ego and the Id*, *ibid.* Vol. VI, pp. 13ff.

35. See Fingarette, *op. cit.* p. 111.

36. David Hume, *A Treatise of Human Nature*, Book I, Part 4, Section 6 (pp. 251ff. in the edition by L.A. Selby-Bigge, Oxford University Press, London, 1958).

37. An early example is discussed by A.L. Samuel in 'Some Studies in Machine Learning, Using the Game of Checkers' (*I.B.M. Journal*, 1959, pp. 210–29).

38. See note 6. All quotes are from the Barnes translation.

39. *Ibid.* p. 48.

40. Jean-Paul Sartre, *L'Éxistentialisme est un humanisme* (Les Editions

Nagel, Paris, 1946); English translation by Philip Mairet, *Existentialism and Humanism* (Methuen, London, 1948).

41. *Being and Nothingness*, pp. 52–3.
42. By K.M. Colby; cf. Margaret Boden, *Artificial Intelligence and Natural Man* (Harvester Press, Hassocks, 1977), pp. 21ff. and bibliography.
43. *Being and Nothingness*, p. 49.
44. See his *Ésquisse d'une théorie des émotions* (Hermann, Paris, 1939); English translation Philip Mairet, *Sketch for a Theory of the Emotions* (Methuen, London, 1962), pp. 66ff.: an early work, but its thesis fits well enough with that of *Being and Nothingness* in this respect.
45. Fingarette, *op. cit.* His page-number references are to the same edition of *Being and Nothingness* as mine.
46. *Being and Nothingness*, p. 68.
47. *Ibid.*
48. *Ibid.* p. 57
49. *Ibid.*
50. *Ibid.* p. 59.
51. *Ibid.* p. 55.
52. *Ibid.* p. 59.
53. Denis Diderot, *Le neveu de Rameau* (ed. R. Desné, Editions Sociales, Paris, 1972); English translation Jacques Barzun, *Diderot: Rameau's Nephew and Other Works* (ed. R. Bowen, Bobbs-Merrill, Indianapolis, 1964).
54. Johan Huizinga, *Homo Ludens: A Study of the Play Element in Culture;* English translation partly by the author, part anonymous: *Homo Ludens* (Paladin, London, 1970), pp. 32–3.
55. *Being and Nothingness*, p. 60.
56. From the song *Werna von Braun* by Tom Lehrer (1965).
57. Hannah Arendt, *Eichmann in Jerusalem*, first published in *The New Yorker* (winter 1962). Cf. Mary McCarthy, 'The Hue and the Cry' in *The Writing on the Wall* (Penguin, 1973), pp. 56ff.
58. See especially Stanley Milgram, *Obedience to Authority: an Experimental View* (Harper & Row, New York, 1974).
59. Arnold Bennett, *Clayhanger* (Eyre Methuen, 1976, p. 416)
60. C.S. Lewis, *The Screwtape Letters* (Fontana, London and Glasgow, 1970), pp. 12–13.
61. *Ibid.* pp. 55–6.
62. Stanley Milgram, *The Individual in a Social World* (Addison-Wesley, Reading, Mass., 1977), p. 113.
63. Thursten B. Brewin, 'The Cancer Patient: Communication and Morale' (*The British Medical Journal*, 1977), pp. 5–6.
64. *Ibid.* p. 6.
65. *Ibid.*
66. Fingarette, *op. cit.*
67. *Ibid.* p. 53.
68. *Ibid.* p. 35.
69. *Ibid.* pp. 38–40.
70. *Ibid.* p. 41.

71. *Ibid.* pp. 69–70; italicized quote in inset *ibid.* p. 69.
72. *Ibid.*, pp. 41–3.
73. *Ibid.* pp. 41–50.
74. *Ibid.* p. 7.
75. *Ibid.* pp. 63–4.
76. *Ibid.* pp. 53–4.
77. John Buchan, *The Thirty-Nine Steps* (Nelson, London, 1951), pp. 80–1.
78. Fingarette, *op. cit.* p. 68.
79. *Ibid.* p. 70.
80. *Ibid.* p. 68.
81. *Ibid.* pp. 72–3.
82. *Ibid.* p. 68.
83. *Ibid.* p. 87.
84. *Ibid.* pp. 86–8.
85. R.D. Laing, *The Dividend Self* (Penguin, 1965), pp. 97–8.
86. Marcel Proust, *À la Recherche du temps perdu* (NRF/Gallimard, Paris, 1954); English translation C.K. Scott Moncrieff and S. Hudson, *Remembrance of Things Past* (Chatto & Windus, London, 1941); Lord Baden-Powell of Gilwell, *Lessons from the 'Varsity of Life* (Pearson, London, 1934).
87. Margaret Lane, *The Brontë Story* (Fontana, London and Glasgow, 1969), pp. 78–9.
88. Fingarette, *op. cit.* pp. 86–7.
89. He mentions in particular K.R. Eissler, Morton M. Gill, and *Psychoanalytic Concepts and the Structural Theory* by J.A. Arlow and C. Brenner (International Universities Press, New York, 1964).
90. Fingarette, *op. cit.* p. 133.
91. Charlotte Brontë, journals and letters quoted in Lane, *op. cit.* pp. 238–9 and 242.
92. *Ibid.* p. 238.
93. *Ibid.* p. 243.
94. Mary McCarthy, *The Group* (Weidenfeld & Nicolson, London, 1963), p. 261.
95. *Being and Nothingness*, pp. 55–6.
96. *Ibid.* p. 56.
97. Hans Christian Andersen, 'The Emperor's New Clothes' (*Andersen's Fairy Tales*, ed. M.O. Osbourne, Hampton, New York, 1930), pp. 283ff.
98. David Wiggins, in an unpublished paper, 'Knowledge, Self-Deception and the Transparency of Consciousness'. I am not sure that he still has this view.
99. William Golding, *Free Fall* (Penguin, 1955), p. 248.
100. 'Tom o'Bedlam's Song', quoted in Robert Graves, *The Crowning Privilege* (Penguin, 1955), p. 248.
101. Anthony Clare, 'Guilty but Insane', (*The Times Literary Supplement*, 14 July, 1968) p. 797.
102 *Ibid.*
103 Compare Kierkegaard's serious/ironic invocation of self-deception, in

the hope of reconciling Socratic Social Worker and Christian Judge:

'Socrates is right: if a man does not do the right, it is because he does not understand it; if he understood it, he would do it — ergo, sin is ignorance.

Christianity is right: sin is guilt. It is quite correct that if a man does not do the right it is because he does not understand it; if he understood it etc. etc. . . . . But he does not understand the right because he is unable to understand the right, and he is unable to understand the right because he does not *want* to understand it — see, here it comes.

Only by treating everything as criminal has Christianity coped with the world and managed to maintain justice.'

Søren Kierkegaard, *Journals and Papers* (ed. H.V. Hong and E.H. Hong, Indiana University Press, 1975), p. 220.

104. See Appendix B.
105. See for example Descartes, *Meditations on First Philosophy*, Meditation I (pp. 145ff. in E. Haldane and G.R.T. Ross, *The Philosophical Works of Descartes*, Vol. I, Cambridge University Press, London, 1969). No claim that Descartes later makes to knowledge can in fact escape his own sceptical traps.
106. Mary McCarthy, *The Company She Keeps* (Penguin, 1966), p. 203ff.
107. Fingarette, *op. cit.* pp. 142–3.
108. Quoted in frontispiece of J. Stolnitz, *Aesthetics* (Macmillan, New York, 1965).
109. Taylor and Martin, *op. cit.*
110. *Ibid.* p. 282.
111. *Ibid.* pp. 219–20.
112. *Ibid.* p. 284.
113. McDougall, *op. cit.*
114. *Ibid.* pp. 541ff.
115. *Ibid.* p. 497.
116. Morton Prince: *The Dissociation of a Personality, op. cit.*
117. Sizemore, *op. cit.*, chapters 15 and 16 (pp. 371ff.).
118. *Ibid.* p. 396.
119. See note 22 above.
120. Sizemore, *op. cit.* p. 413.
121. References in Fingarette, *op. cit.* p. 165.
122. (i) Stuart Dimond, *The Double Brain* (Churchill Livingstone, Edinburgh and London, 1972); (ii) Thomas Nagel, *Mortal Questions* (Cambridge University Press, 1979).
123. Fingarette, *op. cit.* p. 159.
124. *Ibid.* p. 156.
125. *Ibid.* p. 157.
126. *Ibid.* pp. 158–9.
127. *Ibid.* pp. 157–9.
128. Taylor and Martin, *op. cit.* p. 290.
129. See Dimond, *op. cit.* pp. 166–8.
130. Above, p. 38.

131. Plato, *Protagoras* 358 c-d, my translation. Compare *Meno* 78a, and *Gorgias* 468c; also Xenophon, *Memorabilia* III.ix.4 and IV.vi.6, and Aristotle, *Magna Moralia* 1182a20; *Eudemian Ethics* 1216b2ff. and 1144 b 18. My interest here is less in what Socrates in fact said than in how I think the 'paradox' has commonly been taken. For a longer discussion, see the note to the *Protagoras* passage in the translation by C.C.W. Taylor (*Plato: Protagoras*, Clarendon Press, Oxford, 1976), pp. 202ff., and W.K.C. Guthrie, *Socrates* (Cambridge University Press, London, 1971), pp. 130ff.

132. *Protagoras* 358 b.

133. Thomas Love Peacock, *Headlong Hall* (Everyman's Library, London, undated), pp. 83–4. First published 1816.

134. *Ibid.* p. 84.

135. Ovid, *Metamorphoses*, VIII, lines 20–21. (He is following Euripides, *Medea* 1075–1080.) The relevant lines are:

> [Medea:]   . . . Si possem, sanior essem.
> Sed trahit invitam nova vis; aliudque Cupido,
> Mens aliud suadet. Video meliora proboque,
> Detriora sequor.

('I would be saner if I could, but a strange force drives me on against my will. Desire urges me one way, reason another. *I see the better way and approve it; I follow the worse.*' [My italics])

136. For a longer discussion of the paradoxes, with Greek texts and English translations, see G.S. Kirk and J.E. Raven, *The Presocratic Philosophers* (Cambridge University Press, London, 1957), pp. 286ff.; bibliography p. 448.

137. *Ibid.* p. 294.

138. Xenophon, *op. cit.* I.iv.4 ff., IV.iii.3 ff.

139. *Phaedo* 97 c-d, tr. Hugh Tredennick in E. Hamilton and H. Caines (eds.), *The Collected Dialogues of Plato* (Pantheon, New York, 1961), p. 79. Anaxagoras disappointed Socrates:

> As I read on I discovered that the fellow made no use of mind . . . but adduced causes like air and aether. . . . It seemed to me that he was just about as inconsistent as if someone were to say, the cause of everything that Socrates does is mind — and then, in trying to account for my several actions, said first that my body is composed of bones and sinews . . . [etc.] and since the bones move freely in their joints, the sinews by relaxing and contracting enable me somehow to bend my limbs, and that is the cause of my sitting here [in prison] . . . and never troubled to mention the real reasons, which are that since Athens has thought it better to condemn me, therefore I for my part have thought it better to sit here. . . .
> (*Ibid.* 98 b-d, p. 80.)

140. *Timaeus* 29 c-d. The Demiurge is not a creator but an arranger, and is not omnipotent: nature (unlike the Forms which are the Demiurge's

model) does not allow perfect order. But what order there is, is due to
him.

141. *Ibid.* 29 e.
142. Stanley Milgram, *op. cit.* p. 6.
143. Isaiah Berlin, *Four Essays on Liberty* (Oxford University Press, London
     and New York, 1969), pp. xi-xii.
144. *Ibid.* p. xvii.

SHORT BIBLIOGRAPHY

Aristotle, *Eudemian Ethics; Nichomachean Ethics* (in English in the Oxford Translation, eds. J.A. Smith and W.D. Ross, Oxford University Press, London, 1908–52)

Boden, Margaret, *Artificial Intelligence and Natural Man* (Harvester Press, Hassocks, 1977)

Demos, Raphael, 'On Lying to Oneself' (*The Journal of Philosophy*, September 1960)

Dimond, Stuart, *The Double Brain* (Churchill Livingstone, Edinburgh and London, 1972)

Fingarette, Herbert, *Self-Deception* (Routledge & Kegan Paul, London, 1969)

Frankel, Fred H., *Hypnosis: Trance as a Coping Mechanism* (Plenum, London & New York, 1976)

Freud, Sigmund, *The Standard Edition of the Complete Psychoanalytic Works* (eds. J. Strachey and A. Freud, Hogarth Press, London, 1953–66)

Guthrie, W.K.C., *Socrates* (Cambridge University Press, London, 1971)

Hamlyn, D.W. and Mounce, H.O., 'Self-Deception' (*The Aristotelian Society, Supplementary Volume*, 1971)

Kierkegaard, Søren, *Journals and Papers* (eds. H.V. and E.H. Hong, Indiana University Press, 1975)

McDougall, William, *Outline of Abnormal Psychology* (Methuen, London, 1926)

Milgram, Stanley, *Obedience to Authority: an Experimental View* (Harper & Row, New York, 1974); *The Individual in a Social World* (Addison-Wesley, Reading, Mass., 1977)

Nagel, T., 'Brain Bisection and the Unity of Consciousness' (*Mortal Questions*, Cambridge U.P., 1979)

Pears, David, 'The Paradoxes of Self-Deception' (*Questions in the Philosophy of mind*, Duckworth, London, 1975)

Plato, *Gorgias; Meno; Protagoras* (all in English in *The Collected Dialogues of Plato*, eds. E. Hamilton and H. Caines, Pantheon, New York, 1961)

Prince, Morton, *The Dissociation of a Personality: a biographical study in abnormal psychology* (Longmans, New York, 1905); *The Unconscious: the fundamentals of human personality normal and abnormal* (Macmillan, New York, 1921)

Sartre, Jean-Paul, *Being and Nothingness* (tr. Hazel E. Barnes, Methuen, London, 1957); *Existentialism and Humanism* (tr. Philip Mairet, Methuen, London, 1948); *Sketch for a Theory of the Emotions* (tr. Philip Mairet, Methuen, London, 1962)

Sizemore, Chris Costner, with Elen Sain Petillo, *I'm Eve* (Jove/Harcourt Brace Jovanovich, New York, 1978)

Szabados, Béla, 'Wishful Thinking and Self-Deception' (*Analysis*, 1973)

Taylor, W.S. and Martin, M.F., 'Multiple Personality' (*The Journal of Abnormal and Social Psychology*, 1944)

Thigpen, C.H. and Cleckley, H., 'A Case of Multiple Personality' (*The Journal of Abnormal and Social Psychology*, January 1954); *The Three Faces of Eve* (Popular Library, New York, 1961)

Williams, Bernard, *Problems of the Self* (Cambridge University Press, London, 1973)

INDEX OF PROPER NAMES
AND PSEUDONYMS

'A' (dissociated personality), *see* 'BCA'
'Alain', 54
Anaxagoras, 145, 145n139
Andersen, H. C., 118, 118n97
Arendt, H., 71n57
Aristotle, 142n131, 157
Arlow, J.A., 104n89, 157
Ayer, A.J., 12, 12n10

'B' (case of post-hypnotic suggestion), 38–41, 46–51, 65, 141
'B' (dissociated personality), *see* 'BCA'
'BCA', 28–33, 37, 38, 41–2, 61–2, 101
Baden-Powell, 102, 102n86
Beauchamp, C. ('Sally', 'the Saint', etc.), 34, 34nn25–6, 39, 41, 42n32, 135, 135n115
Bennett, A., 74, 74n59
Berkeley, G., 46
Berlin, I., 147, 148n143, 149n144
'Black, Eve', *see* Sizemore
Boden, M., 55n42, 157
Braun, W. von, 70, 70n56
Brenner, C., 104n89
Brewin, T.B., 87nn63–5, 157
Brontë, C., 102, 102n87, 111–12, 112nn91–3, 118
Brontë, E., 102, 102n87, 111–12, 112nn91–3, 118
Buchan, J., 93n77

Clare, A., 127nn101–2
Cleckley, H., 32n19, 33, 33nn20–2, 34, 34n24, nn26–7, 42n32, 135, 157

Colby, K.R., 55n42

Demos, R., 4, 4n4, 5n5, 59, 80, 89, 157
Diderot, D., 68, 68n53
Dimond, S., 136, 136n122, 140n129, 157

Eichman, A., 71, 71n57, 72
Eissler, K.R., 104n89
Eliot, T.S., 132, 132n108
Euripides, 143n135

Fingarette, H., 4, 4n3, 43n35, 58, 58n45, 78, 89ff, nn66–76, nn74–84, nn88–90, 131, 131n107, 136ff, 136n121, nn123–7, 157
Freud, S., 42, 42n33, 43n34, 45, 53–5, 98, 104–5, 157

Gazzaniga, M.S., 136–7, 136n121, 137n124
Gill, M.M., 104n89
Golding, W., 125, 125n99
Graves, R., 127n100
Grice, P., 12
Guthrie, W.K.C., 142n131, 157

Hamlyn, D.W., 157
Hanna, T., 27n16, 41, 41nn29–30, 134
Heraclitus, 99
Huizinga, J., 68, 69n54
Hume, D., 44, 44n36

'James', 101, 101n85, 103

Kierkegaard, S., 129n103, 157

Kirk, G.S., 143nn136–7

Laing, R.D., 101, 101n85
'Lancaster, Evelyn', *see* Sizemore
Lane, M., 102n87, 112, 112nn91–3
Lehrer, T., 70n56
Lewis, C.S., 75, 75n60, 77n61

McCarthy, M., 71n57, 112–13,
    112n94, 130, 131n106
McDougall, W., 24, 24n11,
    27n16,28nn17–18, 38n28, 39,
    41nn29–30, 42n32, 135–6,
    136nn113–14, 157
Martin, M.F. (and Taylor, W.S.),
    24, 24n12, 25, 25n13, 27n16,
    28n17, 33, 41n29, 133ff,
    nn109–12, 157
Milgram, S., 71n58, 81, 81n62, 147,
    147n142, 157
Mounce, H.O., 157
'MR₁' 'MR₂', *see* Reynolds

Nasrudin, 10
Nightingale, F., 143

Ovid, 143, 143n135

Peacock, T.L., 142, 142n133,
    143n134
Pears, D., 157
Plato, 23, 142nn131–2, 143, 145,
    145nn139–41, 146, 157
Prince, M., 28, 28n17, 35nn25–6,
    135, 135n115, 157
Proust, M., 102, 102n86

Raven, J.E., 143nn136–7

Reynolds, M. ('MR₁' 'MR₂'), 24–8,
    29, 31, 35–6, 39, 41–2, 134, 139
Ryle, G., 12, 12n9

Samuel, A.L., 46n37
Sartre, J–P., 7, 7n6, 53nn38–44,
    nn46–52, n55, 80, 81, 114ff,
    115nn95–6, 128, 157
Shakespeare, W., xii, 11, 11n17,
    117
Sizemore, C.C., ('Evelyn
    Lancaster', 'Eve White'/'Eve
    Black', etc.), 32ff, 33nn20–2,
    n24, nn26–7, 39–42, 42n32,
    46–7, 51, 55–7, 98, 135–6,
    135nn116–17, 136nn118–20, 157
Socrates, 81, 128, 142ff, 142n131
'Sörgel', 42
Stevenson, R.L., 134
Szabados, B., 1, 1nn1–2, 157

Taylor, C.C., 142n131
Taylor, W.S., *see* Martin, M.F.
Thigpen, C.H., 32n19, 33,
    33nn20–22, 34, 34n24, nn26–7,
    42n32, 135–6, 136n118, 157

West, R., 11, 11n8
'White, Eve', *see* Sizemore
Wiggens, D., 120n98
Williams, B., 26, 26n15, 157
Witman, B., 139

'X, Emile', 42
'X, Mrs' ('Susie'), 139
Xenophon, 142n131

Zeno, 143, 143nn136–7

INDEX OF SUBJECTS

Acting (stage etc.), 67, 69–70, 94

Action, 'automatic', 39, 40, 47; relation to s–d, 80ff, 109, 130

Alienation, 67ff

Alternating personalities, 24ff, 39, 41, 134, 139–40

Altruism, 125, 142–3

Ambiguity, in fact/value terms, 146; in modal terms, 144; in verb 'to be', 60ff; in social rituals, 116

Ambivalent feelings, acted out, 116; about self-deceivers, 120, 128ff

Amnesia, 25, 27–8, 33, 38ff, 134, see also dissociation, memory

Analogy, uses and dangers of, 23, 51, 99–100, see also models

Assent/admission, 18ff, 74ff, 100; without words, 78; see also 'spelling-out'

Attractions of s–d and related behaviour, 77, 87, 103, 105

Avowal/disavowal, 96ff, 131–2, 140, see also 'spelling-out'

Bad faith (mauvaise foi), 53ff, 98, 102, 114ff; paradox of, 57–9, 62, 64ff; infinite regress of, 59, 63, 91

Behaviour associated with s–d, 1, 6, 32–3, 38ff, 58, 73, 76, 80ff, 96, 120ff

Being-for-itself (pour soi), 56–7, 70; -for-others (pour autrui), 66ff; -in-itself (en soi, 'being a thing') 60ff; see also consciousness, freedom, transcendence

Belief, and knowledge, 11ff, 19ff; as a disposition, 14ff; buried, 19ff; by choice, 5ff; cognitive or epistemological versus other types, 6, 12, 19–21, 30, 53, 94, 100, 113, 119, 131; distracting oneself from, 5ff, 110; failing to notice, 5ff; role in deception, 8ff, 92; in defining 's–d', 11ff, 82, 92ff, 100

Beliefs, incompatible, 15ff

Biological usefulness of s–d, 85ff, 103–4

'Censor', 41–2

Christianity, 124, 146, 129n103

Co-conscious personalities, 33ff, 47ff

'Cognition-perception' terms, 89ff, see also believe, know

Compulsive behaviour, 30, 72, 76, 81–2, 109, 113, 114, 117, 120ff, see also determinism

Computors/programs, 46, 46n37, 55–7, 55n42

Conscious versus unconscious 'deceiver', 21, 37ff, 53ff, 81–2, 122–3, 138, see also Hylas, Philonous

Consciousness, dissociation of, 36ff, in multiple personality, 24ff; 'false', 128; perception of, 42ff; recognizing, 42ff; 'strong'/explicit versus 'weak', 89ff, see also avowal, spelling-out; translucency of, 35, 50, 53ff

Consistency saved by s–d, 85ff, 96, 104

'Cover-story' in s–d, 91ff, 113

Cynicism, 56, 59, 63, 71–5, 76, 82

'Dangerous' and 'safe' ways of putting a thing, xi, 80ff, 87–8, 106

Daydreams, 43, 75, 82, 102, 106

Deception, 8, 25ff, 51, 73, 92

Defeatism, 66, 126

Defense, 98, 104
Deliberateness of s–d, 10, 18
Delusion, 3, 28
'Denial' of cancer diagnosis, 86–8
Description/representation as a tactic in s–d, 59ff, 80–1
Design/teleology, 144
Determinism, 65, 125, 128, 147ff
Dissociation, 24, 37ff, 81, 101, 138–9
Distress avoided by s–deceivers, 83ff
Duality/split in s–d, 7, 9, 21ff, 29ff, 52, 73, 106

Ego, 42–3, 54–5; and Counter-Ego 104ff, 113
Engagement in the world, 89ff, 131–2, 138
Examples (fictional) of s–d and related behaviour: Betty, 83, 84ff; C (cancer patient) 82ff, 87, 110–12; Col A (demagogue), 12ff; D (drinking man), 38ff, 60ff, 82, 87, 108–10, 126; Doe and Bloggs, 121ff, 127; Emma, 83ff; Hannay (Buchan), 93ff, 104; husband and wife, 109, 117; journalist ('Uncle Henry' story), 2ff; M (s–deceiving mother: Demos), 4ff, 60, 75, 80, 82, 95, 108–10; man who abuses wife at parties, 114; Medea (Ovid), 143ff; Osmond Orgreave (Bennett), 74; pianist, 79; Polly (McCarthy), 112ff; Rameau's nephew (Diderot), 68; S (s–deceiving scientist), 70ff, 82, 102, 105, 130; Sargent, Margaret (McCarthy), 130–1; Screwtape's 'patient' (Lewis), 75, 77, 86; waiter (Sartre), 66ff; woman flirting (Sartre), 66, 114ff
Existentialism, 102, 124, *see also* Sartre

Face-saving, 114ff, 122, 130
Freedom, 56, 60, 64ff, 72, 81
Freudian slips, 54, 105

Games, 115ff

Guilt (feeling), 103, 105–6, 125

Hallucination, 3–4, 34, 139
'Hylas', 37ff, 55, 58, 95, 104
Hypnosis, 34, 37ff, 44, 65–6, 133, 141
Hypocrisy, 18, 20

Id, 42, 128, *see also* Ego and Counter-Ego, Unconscious
Imagination, 18, 68–9, 79, 84, 94
Impulse, 4–5
Inarticulacy, 62, 64, 71–2
Inscrutability of s–deceivers, 1, 32ff, 71–2, 73, 79–80, 86, 117ff, 120ff, 132
Intent, 80ff, 97, *see also* action
Intraconsciousness, 28, 33, 39–40, 134
Introspection, 43–4, 66
Irony, 69, 74
Irrationality taken as sign of compulsion, 125–6; *see also* perversity, reasonable/realistic standards

Jokes in s–d, 69, 74, 77–8, 91, 114
'Judge', viii, 120ff; 'Judge's Rule', 147ff

Knowledge, and belief, *see* belief; and responsibility, *see* 'Judge's Rule'; Buried *versus* free, 13ff, 16ff, 26–7, 34–5, 39, 55, 61, 74, 76, 80, 91, 94, 99, 109, 111, 129–30, 132, 142; cognitive/ epistemological *versus* other kinds, 12, 21; dispositional, 9, 14ff, 94; role in defining 'deceive', *see* deception; role in s–d, 11ff, 82ff, 92ff, 99–100; 'where not to look', 3, 6–7, 43, 108, *see also* 'means to an end'; valued for itself, 130

Lying (to others), 38, 44, 63, 71, 108ff, 121ff, *see also* pretending

McNaughton Rules, 127
Madness *versus* s–d, 3–4, 124

'Means to an end' pattern of s–d, 2–3, 74, 80, 109ff, 128, *see also* strategy Memory, as criterion of past consciousness, 43–4, 48–50; as criterion of personal identity, 98; dissociation of, in hypnosis, 37ff; in multiple personality, 24ff; dissociation/loss of in s–d, 2, 5, 28ff, *see also* repression; of past s–d, 72–3, 120

Mental Health Act (England 1959), 127

'Mental' *versus* 'physical', 45–6

Metaphor/figure of speech, 's–d' as, 8, 18, 36, 52, 92ff, 120ff; used by s–deceivers, 77, 91, *see also* jokes

Models (for s–d etc.), 23, 46ff, 96, 99–100

Moral, attitudes appropriate to s–d, 120ff; status of suppressed topic in s–d, 104ff; *versus* factual judgments in s–d, 30–2, 70–2

Multiple personality, 24ff, 41–2, 98, 133ff, 139–40

Negligence, 2

Non-contradiction, law of, 17, 64, *see also* paradox

Obsession in s–d, 75, 77, 82, 107

Other people in s–d, 78, 88ff, 108ff, 121ff, 129–30, 132

Paradox, of s–d, 1ff, 8ff, 29, 32–3, 57ff, 80, 89, 91ff, 108, 110, 120ff; Socratic, 81, 128, 142ff

'Person' (*versus* 'individual'), 70, 96ff, 112, 131, 137–8

Personal identity, constituted by avowal, *see* 'person'; different conditions for different people, 101ff; s–d a defense of, 96, 100ff, 131–2

Perversity of s–deceivers, 1–2, 4, 28, 116, 124, 130

'Philonous', 37ff, 53, 58, 104, 135

Play, 68ff, 113, *see also* games

Post-hypnotic suggestion, 38ff, 46ff, 65, 141

Pretending, 50, 108ff, 121ff

Propositions, letters for xi–ii; in defining 'deceive', 1, 8ff

Psychoanalysis, 42ff, 54, *see also* Freud; Fingarette's thesis a branch of, 104ff

Punishment, 124

Rationalizing, 38, *see also*' cover-story'

Reasonable/realistic thinking abandoned in s–d, 32, 128ff

Referential opacity and s–d, xi

Regression, s–d as, 98–9

Repression, 5–6, 41–2, 54, 57–8, 64, 72, 77, 118, 121ff, *see also* buried belief, buried knowledge

Responsibility, and knowledge, *see* 'Judge's Rule'; and s–d, 4, 8, 24, 59, 69–70, 120ff

Role-playing/social ritual, 66ff, 74, 100, 116

'Self-', reflexive, 23, 36, 51–2, 73

Sincerity, 12, 14, 61, 92ff, 97, 108, 124

Skill, as model for s–d, 89ff; *see also* 'spelling-out'

'Social Worker', viii, 120ff, 131, 133

'Spelling-out', 89ff, 137, 140–1, *see also* avowal, 'strong' consciousness

Split-brain, as model for s–d, 136ff

Strategy of s–d, 1ff, 73ff, 130, *see also* means to an end

Suggestibility, 110, 118

Superstition, 112ff

Tactics in s–d, 74ff, 92, 109, 130

Transcendence (*versus* facticity), 60ff, 115

Unconscious thought/action, 42ff, *see also* 'Hylas'

Volition-action terms, 89ff

Wishful thinking, 1–2, 28, 59, 63–4, 66, 72, 87, 111, 118, 129, 146–7, 149